U.S. CONSTITUTION
FOR BEGINNERS®

U.S. CONSTITUTION
FOR BEGINNERS®

BY STEVE BACHMANN • ILLUSTRATIONS BY JORGE DÍAZ

FOR BEGINNERS®

For Beginners LLC
155 Main Street, Suite 211
Danbury, CT 06810 USA
www.forbeginnersbooks.com

ACKNOWLEDGMENTS

Thanks old and new to Glenn Thompson, Dan Simon, Ann Shields, Danny O. Snow, Kim Huff, David and Ellen Bachmannhuff, Dawn Reshen-Doty, Merrilee Warholak, and Joseph Benedict.

CONTENTS

SELECTIVE CHRONOLOGY

1215—Magna Carta

1606—First Charter of Virginia

1620—Mayflower Compact

1639—Fundamental Orders of Connecticut

1641—Massachusetts Body of Liberties

1647—The First Agreement of the People, 1647

1649—Maryland Toleration Act

1688—Glorious Revolution
      1689—English Bill of Rights

1776—Declaration of Independence

1777—Articles of Confederation

1786—Shays' Rebellion

1787—Constitutional Convention

1788—Constitution Ratified

1791—Constitution's Amendment with Bill of Rights

1794—Whiskey Rebellion

1798-1799—Alien & Sedition Acts, Virginia and Kentucky Resolutions

1800—Jefferson's "Revolution"

1803—Federalists' *Marbury v. Madison*

1814-1815—Hartford Convention

1823—*Johnson v. M'Intosh*

1837—Jacksonians' *Charles River Bridge v. Warren Bridge Co.*

1846-1848—Mexican American War

1849—Thoreau, *Civil Disobedience*

1857—*Dred Scott*

1860-1865—Civil War

1868—14th Amendment (equal protection)

1868—Impeachment trial of Pres. Andrew Johnson

1873—*Slaughterhouse Cases*

1877—Compromise of 1877, ending Reconstruction in the South

1886—*Santa Clara County v. Southern Pacific Railroad Company* (corporations are people too)

1896—*Plessy v. Ferguson*

1905—*Lochner v. New York*

1908—*Adair v. U.S., Loewe v. Lawlor*

1913—16th and 17th Amendments (income tax, direct election of Senators)

1919—*Schencks v. U.S., Abrams v. U.S.*

1920—18th and 19th Amendments (prohibition, women get the right to vote)

1929—Stock Market Crash

1932—New Deal

1935—Second New Deal

1937—Judicial Revolution

1944—FDR proposes Second Bill of Rights

1944—*Korematsu v. U.S.*

1947—National Security Act

1954—*Brown v. Board of Education*

1961—Eisenhower's farewell address: "military industrial complex"

1964, 1965, 1966—24th Amendment, Civil Rights Act, Voting Rights Act

1972, 1973—Title IX, *Roe v. Wade*

1971, 1973—Nixon bombs Cambodia, overthrows Allende in Chile

1972-1974—Watergate affair, culminating in Nixon resignation

1983-1987—Grenada, Lebanon, Nicaragua, Irangate

1989, 1991—Invasion of Panama, Gulf War

1998-1999—Impeachment and acquittal of President Bill Clinton

2000—*Bush v. Gore*

2001—September 11, Patriot Act

2002—Iraq, Afghanistan

2008—Worldwide economic crash, election of Barack Obama

2010—*Citizens United v. FEC*

2023—100th birthday of the Equal Rights Amendment (for women)

2028—year when *Grutter v. Bollinger* (2003) says affirmative action should no longer be legal

THE U.S. CONSTITUTION'S ANTECEDENTS

INTRODUCTION

A constitution is a written declaration of society's basic rules. These rules do not drop from the sky. The words—and how those words are interpreted—result from people arguing and fighting over who can do what to whom, which translates into issues like slavery, taxation, the power of corporations, the right to vote, the right to join real labor unions, and more. Thus a constitution should be seen as a "truce" that people draw up in the course of social conflict. The United States Constitution—like a lot of things—is best understood in the context of people struggling in history.

king John

MAGNA CARTA

The first constitution in the English-speaking world was the MAGNA CARTA. It appeared in England when a group of barons got tired of the way King John was ruling the realm. Besides messing with Robin Hood (which was probably fine with the barons anyway), John forced the barons to give him tax money—and worse, service in the army—for ridiculous military adventures overseas. In 1215, the barons took control of London, and forced John to meet with them in a meadow called Runnymeade. There, John agreed to a list of rules he would obey in running the Kingdom. This list became known as the Magna Carta.

> *38. Henceforth no bailiff shall put anyone on trial by his own unsupported allegation, without bringing credible witnesses to the charge.*

39. *No free man shall be taken or imprisoned or disseized or outlawed or exiled or in any way ruined, nor will We go or send against him, except by the lawful judgment of his peers or by the law of the land.*

40. *To no one will we sell, to no one will we deny or delay right or justice.*

It appears that John intended to break the Magna Carta agreement as soon as he had the power to do so. However, he died the next year, and his young son Henry (the Third) was in no position to fight with the barons over the Magna Carta. The English came to see it as the primary list of rules for living in the kingdom.

EARLY CONSTITUTIONS

When English people started living in North America, they set up rules for living in the new land. Usually they did this on the basis of a charter granted by the king, like the VIRGINIA CHARTER. (The point, in part, was to clarify who owned what and who owed what to whom.) Or they would make one up themselves, if they could, which is what the Pilgrims did in Massachusetts. Documents like the Virginia Charter and the MAYFLOWER COMPACT were early constitutions.

FIRST CHARTER OF VIRGINIA, April 10, 1606:

Also we do, for Us, our Heirs, and Successors, DECLARE, by these Presents, that all and every Persons being our Subjects, which shall dwell and inhabit within every or any of the said several Colonies and Plantations, and every of their children, which shall happen to be born within any of the Limits and Precincts of the said several Colonies and Plantations, shall HAVE and enjoy all Liberties, Franchises, and Immunities, within any of our other Dominions, to all Intents and Purposes, as if they had been abiding and born, within this our Realm of ENGLAND, or any other of our said Dominions.

William Brewster

MAYFLOWER COMPACT, NOV. 11, 1620:

We, whose names are underwritten... Do by these Presents, solemnly and mutually, in the Presence of God and one another, covenant and combine ourselves together into a civil Body Politics, for our better Ordering and Preservation, and Furtherance of the Ends aforesaid: And by Virtue hereof do enact, constitute, and frame, such just and equal Laws, Ordinances, Acts, Constitutions, and Offices, from time to time, as shall be thought most meet and convenient for the general Good of the Colony....

REASONS FOR EMIGRATION

The seventeenth century saw English people leaving merrie olde England to live in North America because England wasn't so merrie anymore.

Queen Elizabeth I

The centuries after Magna Carta had seen your regular array of royal assassinations, baronial rebellions, and peasant riots. The Magna Carta was seldom an issue, though, either because people had other things to fight over, or because the kings were so strong that they could force their interpretation of Magna Carta down the throats of everyone else.

In the 1600s, however, all this began to change, particularly when the Stuart family assumed the throne of England after the death of Queen Elizabeth in 1603.

Religion provided a major source of tension. In the 1500s, most of England had become Protestant, but for a few years, Elizabeth's older sister Mary had tried burning English people to force them to return to Catholicism. After Mary's death, the English remained nervous because they saw the Catholics pushing thought control in Spain (the Inquisition), mass killings in France (Batholomew Day Massacre) and military conquest in Germany (Thirty Years War).

Queen Elizabeth was no Queen Mary. She made sure her people thought she loved and respected them. She had impeccable Protestant credentials. More importantly, Elizabeth knew how to deal with aggressive Catholics from powerful Spain. When Spain sent an Armada to invade England, Elizabeth sunk the ships with the help of her good people and God's bad weather.

Elizabeth was a hard act to follow, and the Stuarts made things even harder. King James Stuart I and his son, Charles I, were snots. They liked their religion with a degree of pomp (which outraged the Puritans who liked their Protestantism "pure"). James and Charles also sucked up to Catholic powers like Spain and France.

English people who were nervous about prelates controlling their worship and rulers grabbing their money left England for North America.

King James I

REVOLUTION
IN ENGLAND

Not every malcontent left England. As quickly as they left, King James's successor, Charles, created more of them. Not only did he marry a Catholic wife, he was even more aggressive than his father in telling the Puritans that they could not worship like Puritans. Worse, he began levying taxes without the consent of Parliament. (Parliament was a body which represented the well-to-do in the Kingdom, and the King was supposed to get consent from this group before he took money from them.) Finally, Charles started throwing people who did not pay his illegal taxes into jail.

Much of what Charles did seemed to violate the provisions of the Magna Carta. When Parliament protested, Charles stopped calling Parliament into session. When people tried to take these issues to court, the judges (appointed by the King) said that what Charles did was OK because he was the king, and the king had to be obeyed or there would be no social stability, no national security, and so forth and so on.

"THE LAW IS IN ITSELF AN OLD TRUSTY SERVANT OF THE KING'S; IT IS HIS INSTRUMENT OR MEANS BY WHICH HE USETH TO GOVERN HIS PEOPLE BY." SIR ROBERT BERKELEY JUSTICE OF THE KING'S BENCH

KING CHARLES I

BRITISH LAW

Charles managed well enough until 1639, when he tried to tell the Scots how to worship. They raised an army that overran Charles' forces. Charles had to call Parliament in order to raise money for more and better troops. Parliament wanted to talk about the rights Charles had been violating before they gave him money or soldiers. To push the members of Parliament to his way of thinking, Charles tried to arrest some of them in the House of Commons. But Parliament raised its own troops and turned on the king. England was plunged into civil war.

CHARLES

° °VS ° °

CAVALIER   ROUNDHEAD

PARLIAMENT

Parliament's army beat the pants off Charles' troops because Parliament was willing to let ordinary people serve in positions normally filled by aristocrats. To the surprise of the aristocrats, the ordinary people had a lot of military talent and determination. By 1647, some of the more politically active commoners in the army thought it was time for them to determine how the country would be run after the revolution. A group of them began drafting a series of documents which would have been the first official constitution for England. This group was called the Levellers, because they wanted a more equal ("leveled") distribution of power.

THE FIRST AGREEMENT OF THE PEOPLE, October 28, 1647:

1. *That matters of religion and the ways of God's worship are not at all entrusted by us to any human power...*

2. *That the matter of impresting and constraining any of us to serve in the wars is against our freedom...*

3. *That after the dissolution of this present Parliament, no person be at any time questioned for anything said or done in reference to the late public differences...*

4. *That in all laws made or to be made every person may be bound alike...*

5. *That as the laws ought to be equal, so they must be good, and not evidently destructive to the safety and well-being of the people.*

REVOLUTIONARY COLONY CONSTITUTIONS

In the meantime, the English people in the colonies were not sitting idle. They too, drafted constitutions and declarations of rights.

THE FUNDAMENTAL ORDERS OF CONNECTICUT (1639):
...well knowing where a people are gathered the word of God requires that to maintain the peace and union of such a people there should be an orderly and decent government ... [we] do therefore associate and conjoin ourselves to be as one public state or commonwealth... also in our civil affairs to be guided and governed according to such law, rules, orders and decrees as shall be made, ordered and decreed, as follows...

MARYLAND TOLERATION ACT (1649):
...noe person or persons whatsoever within this Province ... professing to believe in Jesus Christ, shall from henceforth bee any waies troubled, Molested or discountenanced for or in respect of his or her religion...

MASSACHUSETTS BODY OF LIBERTIES, December 10, 1641:
1. No man's life shall be taken away, no man's honor or good name shall be stained, no man's person shall be arrested, restrained, banished, dismembered, nor any ways punished... unless it be by virtue or equity of some express law of the country warranting the same...
2. Every person within this jurisdiction, whether inhabitant or foreigner, shall enjoy the same justice and law...
47. No man shall be put to death without the testimony of two or three witnesses, or that which is equivalent there unto.

13

48. *Every Inhabitant of the Countrie shall have free libertie to search and veewe any Rooles, Records, or Regesters of any Court or office except the Councel...*

80. *Every married woman shall be free from bodily correction or stripes by her husband, unless it be in his own defense upon her assault....*

89. *If any people of other nations professing the true Christian religion shall flee to us from the tyranny or oppression of their persecutors, or from famine, wars, or the like necessary and compulsory cause, they shall be entertained and succored amongst us, according to that power and prudence God shall give us.*

COUNTER-REVOLUTION TO GLORIOUS REVOLUTION

The Revolution in England went only so far. Parliament executed King Charles, but the Levellers made the richer Parliamentarians nervous. The latter squished the former (at Burford, 1649), and Parliament's general Oliver Cromwell ruled as "Lord Protector." When Cromwell died, the well-to-do thought it would be safer to have a king than mess around further with this democracy stuff. So the son of Charles I was called from France to return to England. Charles II was given the throne on the condition that he listen to the well-to-do in Parliament, pay the army, allow some freedom of religion, and sanction land transactions that had occurred during the Revolution.

When the new Parliament met, the well-to-do started dealing with the less-well-to-do. During the revolution, ordinary people had begun exercising a number of democratic rights, including the right to print local news, and the right to gather signatures in a petition and present them to Parliament. After the Restoration, (of King Charles II) Parliament squelched these rights.

Charles II generally steered clear of any confrontation with Parliament. His brother and successor, James II, was less circumspect. He appointed Catholics to every post he could, and allowed freedom of religion to Catholics and religious dissenters. Catholics were making a lot of English people nervous because in France the Catholic King had just revoked religious tolerance for Protestants (1685). When James II jailed some protesting Anglican bishops for seditious libel, seven rich Englishmen invited William of Orange (King of Netherlands) to invade England. Knowing he had so much Protestant support in England, William found this to be an offer he could not refuse. He sailed an army into England. King James' supporters abandoned him, and he ran away to France.

JAMES II

This was called the GLORIOUS REVOLUTION OF 1688. Some people consider it "glorious" because James did not have his head cut off. Others consider it glorious because it was during this period that Parliament re-established the right to petition. It also allowed the censorship laws to lapse. It formalized the right to *habeas corpus*, which forced jailors to give legal grounds for holding prisoners,

Hebeas Corpus!

and provide valid information as to prisoners' whereabouts, and it also required them to release prisoners who had been unlawfully held.

Another reason this revolution was so glorious was because the following year (1689) Parliament passed a Bill of Rights to confirm and secure what a lot of people had been fighting for:

ENGLISH BILL OF RIGHTS (1689):

5. *That it is the right of the subjects to petition the king, and all commitments and prosecutions for such petitioning are illegal;*

6. *That the raising or keeping a standing army within the kingdom in time of peace, unless it be with consent of Parliament, is against law;*

7. *That the subjects which are Protestants may have arms for their defence suitable to their conditions and as allowed by law;*

RIGHT TO BEAR ARMS

8.   *That election of members of Parliament ought to be free;*

9.   *That the freedom of speech and debates or proceedings in Parliament ought not to be impeached or questioned in any court or place out of Parliament;*

10. *That excessive bail ought not to be required, nor excessive fines imposed, nor cruel and unusual punishments inflicted;*

TRANSITION

After 1702, the English were about done with charter drafting and rights declarations. If everyone was not totally satisfied, dissatisfaction did not raise people to revolutionary levels as it had in the middle 1600s. The English people in America began to worry more about nearby and hostile French and Indians than they worried about their rulers across the sea.

In 1763, things changed again. England had just won a war with France. England decided it was time to run an empire. For the colonists, this meant (among other things) that they could not steal the Indians' land beyond the Appalachians. Worse, they had to start buying British goods, instead of any goods they fancied. Worse still, they had to pay taxes that Parliament imposed on them without their consent – something Parliament had objected to when King Charles tried it on them 100 years before.

18

DECLARATION OF INDEPENDENCE

The colonists did not like any of this empire stuff. They threw British tea into the Boston Harbor (1773).

There is a dignity, a majesty, a sublimity, in this last effort of the patriots, that I greatly admire. The people should never rise without doing something to be remembered, something notable and striking. This destruction of the tea is so bold, so daring, so firm, intrepid and inflexible, and it must have so important consequences, and so lasting, that I cannot but consider it as an epoch in history. —John Adams

John Adams

19

The British closed the port of Boston, revoked privileges in some colonial charters, and forced colonists to house British soldiers. The colonists started protesting in the streets. They burnt effigies. They boycotted British goods. They set up committees to keep themselves informed of local political and military developments. In 1774, delegates from 12 of the 13 colonies met in a "first continental congress." In April 1775, the British began worrying about military stores that the Massachusetts militia was holding in Concord. When British soldiers marched to seize the supplies American farmers began shooting at them on Lexington Green and Concord Bridge. A second continental congress met and sent George Washington (of Virginia) to raise a people's army in Massachusetts.

The British and Americans grew less and less amused with each other. By July 1776, the delegates in the continental congress issued the DECLARATION OF INDEPENDENCE, declaring themselves free from Britain:

We hold these truths to be self-evident, that all men are created equal, that they are endowed by their Creator with certain unalienable Rights, that among these are Life, Liberty and the pursuit of Happiness.—That to secure these rights, Governments are instituted among Men, deriving their just powers from the consent of the governed,—That whenever any Form of Government becomes destructive of these ends, it is the Right of the People to alter or to abolish it, and to institute new Government, laying its foundation on such principles and organizing its powers in such form, as to them shall seem most likely to effect their Safety and Happiness.

Britain's answer was war, and seven years of fighting began.

STATE CONSTITUTIONS

The Declaration of Independence meant that each colony was suddenly a new nation. Each state began drafting a constitution to set up the principles of government the state would follow.

NEW HAMPSHIRE

NEW YORK

MASSACHUSETTS

RHODE ISLAND

PENNSYLVANIA

CONNECTICUT

NEW JERSEY

DELAWARE

MARYLAND

VIRGINIA

NORTH CAROLINA

SOUTH CAROLINA

GEORGIA

Nor can any man who is conscientiously scrupulous of bearing arms, be justly compelled thereto, if he will pay such equivalent, nor are the people bound by any laws, but such as they have in like manner assented to, for their common good —PENNSYLVANIA

...that a long continuance, in the first executive departments of power or trust, is dangerous to liberty; a rotation, therefore, in those departments, is one of the best securities of permanent freedom—MARYLAND.

That general warrants—whereby an office or messenger may be commanded to search suspected places, without evidence... ought not to be granted—NORTH CAROLINA

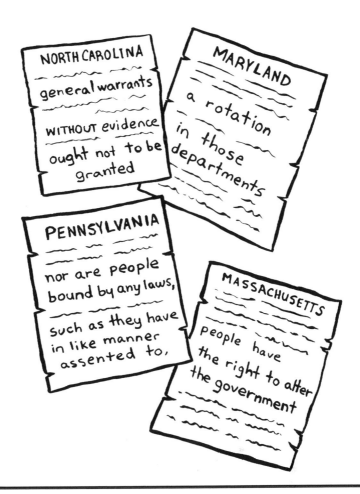

The end of the institution, maintenance, and administration of government, is to secure the existence of the body politic, to protect it, and to furnish the individuals who compose it with the power of enjoying in safety and tranquility their natural rights, and the blessings of life; and whenever these great objects are not obtained, the people have a right to alter the government and to take measures necessary for their safety, prosperity, and happiness—MASSACHUSETTS

REVOLUTION & RIGHTS

While the colonists began governing themselves, they also set to work ridding themselves of counterrevolutionaries. LOYALISTS (those who remained sympathetic to King George) were purged from college faculties, tortured, intimidated, imprisoned, deprived of arms, property, and voting rights. Proportionately almost five times as many people were driven from revolutionary America, than from revolutionary France (1789): the French revolution produced 5 emigres per 1,000, the American, 24...

OUT LOYALISTS

ARTICLES OF CONFEDERATION, PRO AND CON

In the meantime, the new states wanted to remain united. In 1777, they drafted a document called the ARTICLES OF CONFEDERATION, which gave certain limited authority to a national Congress:

> *II. Each state retains its sovereignty, freedom, and independence, and every power, jurisdiction, and right, which is not by this Confederation expressly delegated to the United States, in Congress assembled.*

Under the Articles, the new nation beat the British and won the Revolutionary War (1783). It created a post office and a bureau for foreign affairs. It ended the squabbling between the states over the Western lands and created a policy for the establishment of democratic institutions there. It also demobilized the army, having entered peacetime, to minimize risk of a military takeover of government.

According to the system established by the Articles of Confederation, the national government depended upon the good graces of the states for its income.

Many leaders in the states preferred to keep power in the state capitols (in their own hands) than to give that power up, instead, to a national government. Because of this, the national government set up by the Articles of Confederation was weak.

STATES

federal government

However, there were a number of groups in American society who were not happy with a weak national government. Manufacturers wanted a stronger national government that could pass protective tariffs and create a protected market in all thirteen states. Merchants wanted a stronger national government to establish uniform trade laws. Owners of western lands thought their holdings would be more secure with a stronger federal power. Financiers preferred a uniform national financial system, and did not want the payment of the national debt to depend on the whims of the several states. Creditors were afraid that state legislatures would start printing reams of paper money, and so weaken the value of their holdings.

THE RHODE ISLAND
STATE ARMY

SHAYS'
REBELLION
AND
RHODE ISLAND

WEALTHY
CREDITORS

INDEBTED FARMER
UPRISING

While creditors dreaded the printing of paper money, debtors welcomed it, especially the farmers, who were consistently short of cash.

> *The want of a circulating medium subjects the inhabitants to the greatest inconveniences, the people in general are extremely embarrassed with publick and private debts—no money can be obtained either by the sale or mortgage of real estate.*
>
> *—28 September 1786, from a county convention petition*

Then in 1786 Rhode Island passed a law requiring creditors to accept its paper money at full value. That same year, angry farmers in Western Massachusetts took up arms and began closing the courts to prevent creditors from foreclosing on their lands. The wealthy raised money to help the state government raise an army. This army squished SHAYS' REBELLION (named after one of the farmers' leaders, a revolutionary war veteran unable to pay a $12 debt). Defeated with guns, the farmers went to the ballot box and elected a governor (John Hancock) and a legislature sympathetic to their cause.

REACTION TO SHAYS' REBELLION

The rising of the Shaysites and others in New England shocked a number of "respectable" Americans who worried about the security of their property.

Henry Knox
(Massachusetts Revolutionary War Officer)
To
George Washington
(Revolutionary War Commander):

Their [the Shaysites'] creed is "That the property of the United States has been protected from the confiscations of Great Britain by the joint exertions of all, and therefore ought to be the common property of all… This dreadful situation has alarmed every man of principle and property in New England… Our government must be braced, changed, or altered to secure our lives and property.

George Washington
(Revolutionary War Commander)
to
Henry Lee
(Virginia Revolutionary War Officer):

You talk, my good sir, of employing influence to appease the present tumults in Massachusetts … Influence is no government. Let us have one by which our lives, liberties, and priorities will be secured, or let us know the worst at once…

Thomas Jefferson worried more about the security of democracy:

I hold it that a little rebellion now and then is a good thing. … It is a medicine necessary for the sound health of government. … The tree of liberty must be refreshed from time to time with the blood of patriots and tyrants. It is its natural manure.

—Thomas Jefferson, American Ambassador to France

MAKING THE CONSTITUTION

CONVENTION PRELUDES

The respectable Americans were so upset by these challenges to property they started taking their class interests seriously. Delegates from Virginia and Maryland had met in 1785 to discuss navigation of the Potomac River and the Chesapeake Bay. They called for a more general meeting to take place in Annapolis in 1786, ostensibly to discuss commercial matters. In the end, only five states attended the gathering. The Annapolis delegates called for another convention to take place in 1787.

In the meantime, the national Congress argued over possible amendments to the Articles of Confederation. In early 1787, it called for the states to send delegates to a new convention to consider revisions of the national system.

Had it not been for the eruptions in Rhode Island and Massachusetts, it is not clear that the 1787 convention would have received any more attention than any of the previous meetings. However, the "respectable" Americans were worried. Except for Rhode Island, delegates from every state showed up in Philadelphia.

In the meantime, the French charge d'affaires, Louis Guillaume Otto, was writing to his superiors in Paris, giving them his own perspective on events as they were unfolding:

Even though there are not patricians in America, there can be found certain men known under the label "gentlemen" who, by their rules, by their talents, by their education, by their families or by their position, aspire to a pre-eminence that the people refuse to let them have; and although several of these men have betrayed the interest of their kind to acquire popularity, there exists among them a rapport made stronger by the fact that they all fear the people's efforts to deprive them of their riches, and also by the fact that they are creditors who have thus an interest in making the government stronger and in overseeing the administering of the law. These men ordinarily pay the highest taxes, whereas poor owners escape the vigilance of the collectors. Most of them being merchants, it is important for them that the United States establish a good credit history with Europe by paying back its debts in full, and that they give Congress enough powers to force the people to contribute.

The necessity has now been felt for a long time, my Lord, to give to the Federal Government more energy and vigor, but one can feel as well that the excessive independence granted to the citizens vis-à-vis the states, and the states vis-à-vis Congress, is much too dear to the individuals to be taken away from them without great precautions. The people do not ignore that the natural consequences of a greater power granted to Congress would be a regular collecting of taxes, a severe administration of justice, extraordinary rights on imports, rigorous actions against debtors, and lastly a marked preponderance of rich men and property owners.

CONVENTION OPENS

The "gentlemen" referred to by Otto who attended the Philadelphia Convention consisted of a number of types. There were people like James Madison and Alexander Hamilton, who knew how to get things done:

JAMES MADISON, OPERATIVE:

Delegate to Continental Congress, Virginia House of Delegates, and Annapolis Convention. Helped to draft Virginia Constitution. In constant contact with nearly everyone who mattered during this period. Kept detailed notes of the Constitutional Convention's proceedings, providing historians with extraordinary original source material.

ALEXANDER HAMILTON, OPERATIVE:

Ill-born, well-married, ambitious and cynical. John Adams called him "the bastard brat of a Scotch peddlar." Thomas Jefferson described him as being "Of acute understanding, disinterested, honest, and honorable in all private transactions, amiable in society, and duly valuing virtue in private life, yet so bitched by the British example as to be under thorough conviction that corruption was essential to the government of a nation."

There were national celebrities like George Washington and Benjamin Franklin, who were expected to lend their prestige to the gathering.

GEORGE WASHINGTON, STAR:

Commander in Chief of the victorious revolutionary army. Possibly the wealthiest man in North America.

BENJAMIN FRANKLIN

BENJAMIN FRANKLIN, STAR:

Best selling author (Poor Richard's Almanac). Inventor (Franklin stove, lightning rod), scientist, diplomat, postmaster, librarian, revolutionary.

There were also members of the Society of Cincinnati, a national fraternity of revolutionary army veterans. A number of Americans (including Franklin, Jefferson, and Adams) were concerned that this group might want to establish itself as a new hereditary aristocracy. 27 of the 55 delegates to the convention were members of this organization.

THOMAS JEFFERSON

PATRICK HENRY

Not attending the convention were John Adams, who was representing the United States in England; Thomas Jefferson, who was representing the United States in France; and Patrick Henry, who refused to attend because he "smelt a rat in Philadelphia, tending toward the monarchy."

VIRGINIA PLAN, CHECKS AND BALANCES

The delegates chose to meet in secret. They did not want the press reporting to their constituents back home about the frank discussions they intended to have.

After the convention opened, the representatives from Virginia presented a plan for a new government, drafted by Madison. Borrowing on ideas from the French philosopher Montesquieu, Madison conceived of having three separate branches of government: the legislature to make the laws, the executive to enforce the laws, and the judiciary to interpret

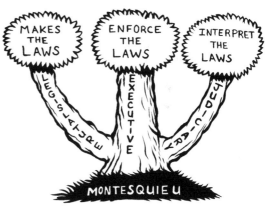

the laws. The aim was to parcel the power out into three distinct branches of government, so that each one might serve as a check on the other.

> ...constant experience shows us that every man invested with power is apt to abuse it, and to carry his authority as far as it will go...
>
> When the legislative and executive powers are united in the same person, or in the same body of magistrates, there can be no liberty; because apprehensions may arise, lest the same monarch or senate should enact tyrannical laws, to execute them in a tyrannical manner.
>
> Again, there is no liberty, if the judiciary power be not separated from the legislative and the executive. Were it joined with the legislative, the life and liberty of the subject would be exposed to arbitrary control; for the judge would then be the legislature. Were it joined to the executive power, the judge might behave with violence and oppression.
>
> —MONTESQUIEU, SPIRIT OF THE LAWS, BOOK XI

ARGUMENTS OVER DEMOCRACY

Under the VIRGINIA PLAN, as it came to be called, the legislature was to consist of two houses, with representatives from each state according to population. Madison included this feature in hopes of securing popular support. The delegates immediately began arguing about democracy. Giving the people political power was fine in theory, but what if they used that power to take property from the rich and spread it around?

> *The people immediately should have as little to do as may be about the government.*
> —Roger Sherman

> *The evils we experience flow from the excess of democracy.* —Elbridge Gerry

> *Men don't unite for liberty or life... They unite for protection of property.*
> —Gouveneur Morris

> *We had been too democratic but were afraid we should incautiously run into the opposite extreme.* —George Mason

> *No government could long subsist without the confidence of the people.* —James Wilson

> *No agrarian attempts have yet been made in this country, but symptoms of a leveling spirit, as we have understood, have sufficiently appeared in certain quarters to give notice of the future danger. How is the danger to be guarded against on republican principles?* —James Madison

WHAT DOES DEMOCRACY MEAN FOR ME?

WHAT CAN IT GUARANTEE?

34

ALTERNATIVES

Another problem with the Virginia Plan was that the small states would be overwhelmed by the bigger states. The smaller states organized together, and on June 15, 1787, they presented what came to be known as the NEW JERSEY PLAN. The New Jersey Plan called for a single legislative body comprised of representatives selected by the state legislatures, with each state having an equal voice.

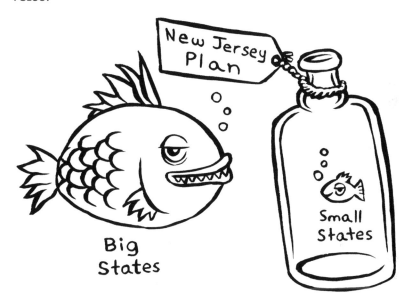

A few days later, Alexander Hamilton presented a plan of his own, based on the British model, offering a "distinct and permanent share in the government" to the "rich and well born" so that they would be able to "check the unsteadiness" of the people. According to Hamilton, "Nothing but a permanent body can check the imprudence of democracy."

GREAT COMPROMISE

At bottom, Hamilton wanted to resurrect the British King and House of Lords in an American version. His plan was so far off in right field that nobody took it seriously. Some observers think the moderates asked Hamilton to proffer such a crazy plan in order to encourage everyone else to settle down and find some compromise.

However, neither the large states nor the smaller states were in any mood for compromise. For weeks the delegates wrangled, but they leaked reports to the press suggesting that everything was going wonderfully within the guarded halls of the convention:

> *So great is the unanimity, we hear, that prevails in the Convention, upon all great federal subjects, that it has been proposed to call the room in which they assemble, UNANIMITY HALL.*

This, of course, was patently false. Various individuals threatened to pack up and go home. Finally, on July 16, the delegates reached what has come to be known as THE GREAT COMPROMISE.

The Great Compromise borrowed ideas from both the Virginia and New Jersey plans. (Hamilton's plan was in the trash bin). Principles of the New Jersey plan were embodied in the provision that the states would be represented equally in one house of the national legislature. The principles of the Virginia plan were embodied in provisions stating that representation according to population would take place in the other house of the national legislature. To placate the Virginia supporters, the delegates also agreed that taxes could originate only in the popular house; a census should be taken every 10 years; and one slave equaled 3/5 of a person. These provisions would eventually lead to the two-member-per-state Senate and the member-by-population House of Representatives.

CONVENTION WRAP UP

After "The Great Compromise," the delegates argued some more, but the intensity and acrimony that preceded The Great Compromise had considerably diminished.

They decided how to elect the President, the Senators, and Representatives, and how to remove them from office. They discussed qualifications for, and terms of, office. They decided how to constitute the Supreme Court.

They decided that slaves could continue to be imported into the nation until 1808.

The national Congress was given the power to "lay and collect taxes," "to regulate commerce with foreign nations, among the several states and with the Indian tribes," and to "declare war." The states were forbidden to "coin money," "impair contractual obligations," or "make anything but gold or silver coin a tender in payment of debts."

Some delegates asked whether or not the Constitution should enumerate a BILL OF RIGHTS, but everybody was tired, and they decided there was no need for a list.

By September 17, 1787, the delegates had completed their final draft of the U.S. CONSTITUTION.

> *It's a Republic, if you can keep it. —Ben Franklin*

AFTER SIGNING

The Constitution that the FRAMERS finally drafted was only a few pages long, consisting of just seven articles. Articles One, Two, and Three dealt with the Legislature, the Executive, and the Judiciary. Article Four covered relations between the states. Article Five dealt with amending the Constitution, and Article Six covered miscellaneous provisions like debts owed by the Confederation, foreign treaties, and qualifications for office. Article Seven declared that only nine states had to ratify the Constitution to bring it into effect (The delegates did not want to have to wait for states like Maryland, which did not ratify the Articles of Confederation until 1781— or Rhode Island, which might never ratify as long as its people believed in paper money).

One reason the document was so concise was that the Framers wanted a flexible instrument that would hold good in the long term. They knew that things change with time, and they wanted the Constitution to be responsive to change. Thus Edmund Randolph, one of the five men charged with drafting the Constitution, observed that "In the draught of a fundamental constitution," it was necessary to

> *insert essential principles only, lest the operations of government should be clogged by rendering those provisions permanent and unalterable, which ought to be accommodated to times and events...*

EDMUND RANDOLPH

> Constitution supporter John Marshall (who later led the Supreme
> Court) would write in a famous opinion that [The Constitution is]
> intended to endure for ages to come, and, consequently, to be
> adapted to the various CRISES of human affairs.

For his part, Thomas Jefferson did not always agree with
the FEDERALISTS (as supporters of the Constitution
came to be called), but he did agree with them that

> ...laws and institutions must go hand in hand with the progress of
> the human mind. As that becomes more developed, more
> enlightened, as new discoveries are made, new truths disclosed, and
> manners and opinions change with the change of circumstances,
> institutions must advance also, and keep pace with the times.

In short, the reality of the Constitution would be found
within the practice of history, and not only within
words set out on paper.

THE FEDERALISTS

JAMES MADISON

THE FEDERALIST

ISSUE #1

COLLECT THEM ALL!

Of course, before the Constitution could develop much meaning in history, it first had to be adopted by the states. As we have seen, the Framers decided that only 9 states would be needed to ratify. Additionally, they stated that ratification should issue from specially-called state conventions, and not state legislatures. Legislatures might have a vested interest in the old ways of doing things, and general elections might be harder to influence than a smaller body of selected delegates.

Having set down ground rules according to their satisfaction, the Federalists then put together one of history's most impressive political campaigns. They issued a number of propaganda pamphlets that came to be known as THE FEDERALIST PAPERS, wherein Hamilton, Madison, and John Jay elaborated political arguments to support ratification of the new Constitution:

EFFICIENCY

Those who have been conversant in the proceedings of popular assemblies... will readily conceive how impossible it must be to induce a number of such assemblies, deliberating at a distance from each other, at different times, and under different impressions, long to co-operate in the same views and pursuits.

FEDERALIST #15 [Hamilton]

And when asked about the legality of the Constitution (which had come from a convention asked only to recommend amendments to the Articles of Confederation), Madison simply adverted to the right of revolution:

ANTI-FEDERALISTS

Not everyone had unqualified enthusiasm for the Constitution, as indicated by various anti-federalist pamphlets:

I had rather be a free citizen of the small republic of Massachusetts, than an oppressed subject of the great American empire...

These violent partisans... consist generally, of the NOBLE order of C[ininnatu]s, holders of public securities, men of great wealth and expectations of public office, [Bankers] and [Lawyers]: these with their train of dependents from the Aristocratick combination.

What then are we to think of the motives and designs of those men who are arguing the implicit and immediate adoption of the proposed government; are they fearful that if you exercise your good sense and discernment, you will discover the masque aristocracy, that they are attempting to smuggle upon you under the suspicious garb of republicanism?

Before MARTIAL LAW is declared to be the supreme law of the land, and your character of free citizens be changed to that of the subjects of a MILITARY KING, which are necessary consequences of the adoption of the proposed constitution, let me admonish you in the name of SACRED LIBERTY, to make solemn pause ... There is not a tincture of democracy in the proposed constitution.

MORE RESERVATIONS

Jefferson's response was mixed:

I like much the general idea of framing a government which should go on of itself peaceably, without needing continual recurrence to the state legislatures.... There are other good things of less moment. I will now add what I do not like. First the omission of a bill of rights providing clearly & without the aid of sophisms for freedom of religion, freedom of the press, protection against standing armies, restriction against monopolies, the eternal & unremitting force of the habeas corpus laws, and trials by jury in all matters of fact triable by the laws of the land & not by the law of nations....Let me add that a bill of rights is what the people are entitled to against every government on earth, general or particular, & what no just government should refuse, or rest on inferences. The second feature I dislike, and greatly dislike, is the abandonment in every instance of the necessity of rotation in office, and most particularly in the case of the President.

Patrick Henry's response was not mixed at all. Believing that individual liberty and not material advantage should be the goal of government, he feared that:

...the American spirit, assisted by the ropes and chains of consolidations, is about to convert this country into a powerful and mighty empire... I dread the operation of it on the middling and lower classes of people: it is for them I hear the adoption of this system...

RATIFICATION

While the arguments went on, the struggle for ratification proceeded. Delaware, New Jersey, Georgia, and Connecticut were all small states with limited resources. They had everything to gain by joining a national union. All four of them ratified the Constitution by mid-January, 1788.

Pennsylvania had ratified a month earlier, but under less auspicious circumstances. There, an assembly with a majority sympathetic to calling a ratifying convention had been due to adjourn on September 29. By hiring a special courier, the Federalists managed to have a copy of the new Constitution delivered by September 28. The following day, Antifederalist legislators vanished from the scene, preventing the assembly from holding a quorum. Undaunted, the Federalists organized a mob of supporters that scoured Philadelphia. Two Antifederalist representatives were found and forced back into the assembly. Provisions for a ratifying convention were "duly" enacted. The Constitution was ratified by its first large state on December 12, 1787.

In February, the ratification movement began to hit snags. In Massachusetts, the Federalists secured an affirmative vote, but not without some upfront and backroom deals. Upfront, the convention recommended that a Bill of Rights be appended to the new Constitution. In the back rooms, the Federalists swayed John Hancock (elected by Shaysites) with the promise that he could be Vice President of the new union; and, if Virginia did not join, he might expect the Presidential office.

FEDERALISTS

ANTI-FEDERALIST

> *Loaves and fishes must bribe the demagogues.*
> *They must be made to expect higher offices*
> *under the general than the state government.*
> *—Gouveneur Morris*

Antifederalist feeling was more intense in New Hampshire, despite its small size. The Federalists found the ratifying convention filled with opponents to the new Constitution. The best they could do, for the time being, was maneuver an adjournment before any decision was made.

In May, Rhode Island—consistent with its rambunctious populism—chose to hold a democratic plebiscite instead of a republican convention. To no one's surprise, the constitution was rejected outright.

While they were losing in New Hampshire and Rhode Island, the Federalists secured the weak states of Maryland and South Carolina in April and May. In the latter state, nearly half the delegates were related to the delegates sent to Philadelphia.

In June, a new convention was held in New Hampshire. This time, the delegates ratified the Constitution, although they followed Massachusetts' example and also recommended amendments.

With New Hampshire, the requisite nine states had ratified. However, without the states of New York and Virginia, the new nation would be a sham.

Virginia debated the Constitution for the entire month of June, and finally ratified with the provision that "the liberty of Conscience and of the Press cannot be cancelled."

New York's delegates were initially opposed to the Constitution. However, the ratification by Virginia, the promise of a Bill of Rights, and the threat that New York City might secede to join the new Union brought New York State into the ratifying column.

North Carolina rejected the Constitution in August.

LEGITIMATION

The precarious success of the Constitution was not lost on the politicians who supported the new government. As the returns showed, those who were asked to give an opinion concerning the Constitution ratified it by only the slimmest of margins. And of course, those who were female, black, or poor, had even less to say. Support for the new order was by no means certain, and there were calls for a second convention. Thus, even while the politicians were prepared for a transfer of power from the Confederation to the Constitution, they took steps to ensure that the new system might receive the greatest support possible.

FIRST, they selected the nation's officers from the two key states, north and south. George Washington from Virginia was made President. Massachusetts was placated by having one of its own elected Vice President—but this individual was John Adams, a fellow more conservative than the Shaysite-supported John Hancock.

46   ~1788~

SECOND, they ensured that as many interests as possible would be represented in the new government. In an early instance of affirmative action, representatives from all over the nation were appointed to the Supreme Court, regardless of whether someone more qualified might have been available (New York, South Carolina, Massachusetts, Pennsylvania, Virginia and North Carolina). George Washington included both the right-wing Alexander Hamilton and the left-wing Thomas Jefferson in his cabinet.

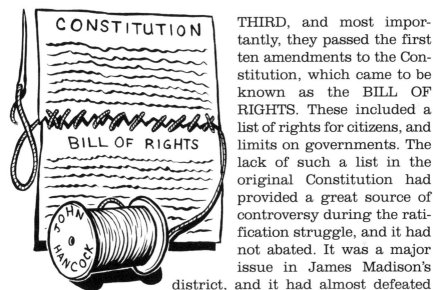

THIRD, and most importantly, they passed the first ten amendments to the Constitution, which came to be known as the BILL OF RIGHTS. These included a list of rights for citizens, and limits on governments. The lack of such a list in the original Constitution had provided a great source of controversy during the ratification struggle, and it had not abated. It was a major issue in James Madison's district, and it had almost defeated him in his bid for a seat in the House of Representatives. When Congress began sitting, he quickly went to work to draft and pass a list of rights which the federal government could not take away.

BILL OF RIGHTS

One important objective of the Bill of Rights was to stop governments from the abuses of power that English-speaking people had known ever since King John.

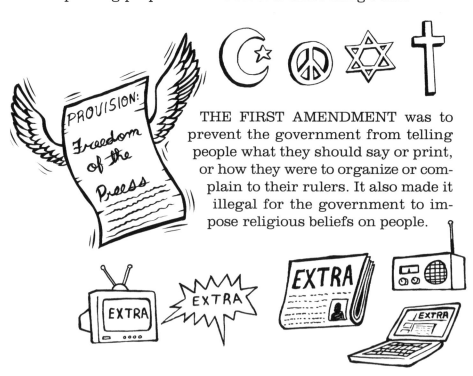

THE FIRST AMENDMENT was to prevent the government from telling people what they should say or print, or how they were to organize or complain to their rulers. It also made it illegal for the government to impose religious beliefs on people.

PROVISION:
Freedom of the Press

THE SECOND AMENDMENT was to prevent the government from taking the ultimate source of political power (and rebellion) from the people: their guns. In feudal society, ordinary citizens were not allowed to bear arms. The Second Amendment reflects the fundamental political insight that a society built on consent (instead of oppression) can afford to have an armed citizenry.

Political power issues from the mouth of a gun. —Mao Zedong

THE THIRD AMENDMENT was designed to prevent the government from forcing citizens to give their homes to soldiers. This had been a common way of housing troops for centuries; it was a big burden for any citizens required to turn their home into a barracks.

THE FOURTH AMENDMENT was to prevent the government from sticking its nose into the personal affairs of the people. It states that before government officials can start arresting people or going through their things, officials would have to have a warrant, based on "probable cause, supported by oath or affirmation, and particularly describing the place to be searched, and the persons or things to be seized."

THE FIFTH AMENDMENT was to prevent the government from using its powers to harass political opponents. If the government wanted to accuse someone of a big crime, it first had to secure the consent of a group of ordinary citizens (the GRAND JURY). If the government lost a trial,

49

it couldn't try the case again (i.e., an accused could not be placed into DOUBLE JEOPARDY). Nor could the government force an accused to testify against him or herself. Nor could the government take any citizen's "life, liberty, or property," without some sort of legal proceeding. Finally, if the government needed someone's property for public use, it would have pay that person "just compensation."

THE SIXTH AMENDMENT set out additional checks on the powers of government, particularly those that related to its capacity to jail people, accuse them, and haul them into court. The Sixth Amendment required that an accused person receive a speedy trial; that he not be tried away from the place where the crime was supposed to have been committed; that he be told why he was being tried; that he be allowed to confront his accusers; that he be allowed to have witnesses presented at the trial to speak for him; and that he be allowed to have a lawyer help him defend himself. In the Sixth Amendment, the American people were looking back to show-trials of Leveller leaders (and looking forward to show-trials of future political dissidents).

THE SEVENTH AMENDMENT was to prevent the government from using establishment-minded judges for railroading people. It guaranteed the right to trial by jury, so that if someone were going to be railroaded, it would be with the consent of some ordinary citizens. (This amendment has had both its happy and adverse effects. In California, a jury acquitted Angela Davis of various charges invented by government prosecutors. In Mississippi, a jury of whites acquitted Klansmen of murdering civil rights workers)

THE EIGHTH AMENDMENT was to prevent the government from squishing people once it had jailed them or secured a guilty plea. It forbade "excessive bail," "excessive fines," and "cruel and unusual punishment." What the Supreme Court thinks of the Eighth Amendment is still open to question. It currently allows corporal punishment for children, and capital punishment for some felons—not to mention deplorable conditions in prisons.

THE NINTH AMENDMENT was intended to ensure that nobody thought the preceding list ended the rights that citizens had against the government: "The enumeration in the Constitution, of certain rights, shall not be construed to deny or disparage others retained by the people." Obviously, the American people were concerned about the extent to which those in power could be corrupted by power (and God knows how often they have been proven right).

THE TENTH AMENDMENT was another "insurance" clause. Powers not given to the central government were reserved "to the States respectively, or to the people." In short, the American people didn't trust the political propriety of the government any farther than they could spit.

Congress began work on the Bill of Rights in 1789. By 1791, the states had ratified it. During this time, North Carolina and Rhode Island finally decided they would join the new system.

The Amendments
of the Bill of Rights

1. FREEDOM OF RELIGION, SPEECH AND OF THE PRESS.
2. RIGHT TO BEAR ARMS.
3. PROHIBITS FORCE QUARTERING
4. PROHIBIT SEARCH WITHOUT WARRANTS. OR PROBABLE CAUSE.
5. RULES FOR INDICTMENT.
6. RIGHT OF SPEEDY TRIAL BY JURY OF PEERS.
7. TRIAL BY JURY IN CIVIL CASES.
8. PROHIBITS EXCESSIVE FINES AND CRUEL-UNUSUAL PUNISHMENT.
9. ASSERTS UNENUMERATED RIGHTS OF THE PEOPLE.
10. LIMITS THE POWERS OF THE FEDERAL GOVERNMENT.

NOT BAD FOR A NEW COUNTRY.

51

ARGUING OVER
THE CONSTITUTION

INTERPRETATION

The constitutional system was in place, but many specific meanings and practical workings had yet to be explained. Perhaps the most controversial question at this point in the nation's history was whether the Constitution should be interpreted broadly or narrowly.

ALEXANDER HAMILTON

FEDERALIST
or
MONARCHIST?

On the broad side of the issue was Alexander Hamilton, who thought that the government should be able to do anything "necessary and proper" to fulfilling its functions. For Hamilton, this meant, among other things, that the new national government could assume the debts of the states, charter a national bank, and pursue an economic policy designed to encourage manufacturers at home. Hamilton's following came to be known as Federalists to their friends, and Monarchists to their enemies.

On the narrow side of the issue were individuals like Thomas Jefferson, who preferred a society with more farmers and less government. Some of his worst fears were confirmed when speculators lined up behind Hamilton's program; and later, when Washington called up an army larger than any he

THOMAS JEFFERSON

REPUBLICAN
or
JACOBIN?

had commanded during the Revolution to crush a tax protest by Pennsylvania farmers (known as the Whiskey Rebellion). Jefferson's following came to be known as Republicans to their friends. Their enemies called them Jacobins, after the groups committing violent revolution in France.

The question of how to properly interpret the Constitution naturally led to a second question: who finally decided what the Constitution meant if people in the government disagreed over it?

For a while, the question was answered by bald practice. Washington usually listened to Hamilton, and Washington was too popular to oppose. This went on for eight years.

THE STATES RESPOND
11TH AMENDMENT

In 1796, John Adams was elected President, and in 1798 he and his Federalists were concerned about winning the next election. They passed the ALIEN AND SEDITION ACTS, which outlawed any "false, scandalous and malicious" utterance or writing against the government or its officials. Only Republicans (no Federalists) were indicted, including newspapermen, a Congressman from Vermont, and one worthy citizen who was heard voicing the hope that a cannon salute might hit the President in his can. While various Federalist judges were sustaining these acts, Jefferson and Madison induced the legislatures of Virginia and Kentucky to pass resolutions claiming for the states the right to invalidate unconstitutional legislation. The Eleventh Amendment, ratified during this period, further increased state power by refusing the right of citizens from one state to sue another state directly. In response to the Virginia and Kentucky Resolutions, many Northern states passed their own declarations, stating that authority to pass on federal laws lay with the Supreme Court.

THE 11th AMENDMENT STRENGTHENED THE INDIVIDUAL STATES BY MAKING THEM IMMUNE TO OUT OF STATE LAWSUITS. A WIN FOR REPUBLICANS.

THE REVOLUTION OF 1800
12TH AMENDMENT

JEFFERSON'S ELECTION IN 1800 WAS COMPLICATED. THE TWELFTH AMENDMENT OF 1803 MADE IT SO THAT THE ELECTORS VOTED FOR BOTH PRESIDENT AND VICE PRESIDENT.

BEFORE THAT THE RUNNER UP TO PRESIDENCY WAS DECLARED THE VICE.

ELECTORAL BALLOT
PRESIDENT?
- - - - - - - -
VICE PRESIDENT?
- - - - - - - -

In the end, the question was resolved, like so many, by political struggle. In 1800, the Republicans won the election, but the choice for President had to be made in the House of Representatives because they hadn't gotten their candidates straight. The Twelfth Amendment was passed to care for this problem henceforth, with electors being required to vote for a President and for a Vice President rather than for two choices for President.

After Thomas Jefferson was elected, he did what he could to reverse the Alien and Sedition Acts. They had been designed to dissolve on the day of the next President's inauguration anyway, and Jefferson ensured that those who had been imprisoned were released, and those who had been fined received refunds.

The Republicans' REVOLUTION OF 1800 included an assault on the Federalist judiciary, whose interpretation of the Constitution had proven so noxious.

> *[The Federalists] have retired into the Judiciary*
> *as a stronghold... and from that battery all the*
> *works of Republicanism are to be beaten down*
> *and erased. —Thomas Jefferson*

The Republicans repealed the Federalists' Judiciary Act of 1801, which would have allowed for the appointment of more Federalist judges, and they redefined the Supreme Court's term so as to prevent it from holding hearings as to the repeal's constitutionality until 1803. The Republicans also began impeachment proceedings against a notorious Federalist judge who was guiltier of drunkenness and insanity than he was of treason, bribery, or high crimes and misdemeanors. They dumped him anyway, and then moved against Supreme Court Justice Samuel Chase, who had howled against the Jeffersonian "mobocracy." This impeachment effort failed, but Chase watched his mouth ever after.

In an attempt to thwart the Republicans, some Federalists tried filing various test cases in hopes of securing judicial invalidation of the Republicans' measures. Their hopes were disappointed by John Marshall, a Federalist recently appointed by John Adams to head the Supreme Court. Yet while Marshall yielded battles to the Republicans, he was laying the groundwork for winning the war.

MARBURY V. MADISON

For Marshall, winning the war did not mean returning all political power to the Federalists. Given the state of the country, that would have been impossible. What was possible, though, was an increase in power for the federal judiciary. Because its members were appointed for life—and because most of them at that point were Federalists—the federal judiciary held the potential for serving as a conservative brake on Jefferson and his "radicals."

JOHN MARSHALL:

John Marshall

Distant cousin and political foe of Thomas Jefferson, who called him "that gloomy malignity." Marshall explained that his nationalist sentiments derived from his experience as a youth during the Revolution. "I had grown up at a time when love of the union and resistance to the claims of Great Britain were the inseparable inmates of the same bosom... when the maxim united we stand, divided we fall was the maxim of every orthodox American; and I had imbibed these sentiments so thoroughly that they Constituted a part of my being."

The question, though, was how to assert the judiciary's power without inviting more reprisals from the Republicans in the legislative and executive branches. The case of *Marbury v. Madison* provided John Marshall with his opportunity. As every law student knows, *Marbury v. Madison* involved the first time the Supreme Court asserted it could declare an act of Congress to be unconstitutional. As every law student may not know, *Marbury v. Madison* also constituted a shrewd political ploy.

The case grew out of the Federalists' last ditch efforts to cram judicial offices with Federalists before they lost power in 1801. William Marbury was one Federalist appointed by John Adams to fill a Justice of the Peace slot in the District of Columbia. However, the appointment had been made so late, that John Marshall (at that time Adams' Secretary of State) did not have time to deliver to Marbury his papers of commission.

The new Secretary of State was the Republican James Madison, and when Marbury came for his paper, Madison told Marbury to jump in a lake—or something like that. Marbury sued.

THE DECISION

In 1803, the Supreme Court had its first chance to rule on Marbury's case. Marshall—who probably shouldn't have heard the case to begin with, because Marbury's plight was partially Marshall's fault—wrote a decision that gave with one hand and took with another. On the one hand, he said that Marbury could not get his commission, and this suited the Republicans just fine. On the other hand, he laced his opinion with snide remarks about the Republican administration. Most importantly, Marshall said that Marbury could not get his papers because he had come to the Supreme Court on the basis of a Congressional law which contravened the Constitution. Of course, to do this, Marshall had to assert the Supreme Court's power to place its interpretation of the Constitution over Congress':

So if a law be in opposition to the Constitution... the court must determine which of these conflicting rules govern the case. This is of the very essence of judicial duty.

Thus, while Marshall managed to avoid a confrontation with the Republicans, he also managed to reserve power in the judicial branch, which might eventually use *Marbury v. Madison* to restrain Republican excesses. Some Republicans might not have worried, but Jefferson did:

> *I long wished for a proper occasion to have the gratuitous opinion in Marbury v. Madison brought before the public, and denounced as not law....*

MARSHALL

LEADING THE SUPREME COURT I HELPED INTERPRET THE LAW IN FAVOR OF THE FEDERALISTS. THE VISION OF RIGHT OF CONTRACT PROPERTY AND NATIONAL POWER.

When *Marbury v. Madison* was rendered, it was probably more significant for the judicial power it preserved than for any new judicial power it created. As we shall see, neither the President nor the states nor the people gave up their rights to determine what the Constitution meant.

Nevertheless, through the next 34 years that he sat on the bench, Marshall quietly but decisively enhanced the Supreme Court's power to interpret the Constitution.

Procedurally, he encouraged the Court to speak only through one Justice (usually himself), which lent more force to Court opinion. Jefferson remarked:

Another most condemnable practice of the supreme court to be corrected is that of cooking up a decision in Caucus & delivering it by one of their members as the opinion of the court, without the possibility of our knowing how many, who, and for what reasons each member concurred.

An opinion is huddled up in conclave perhaps by a majority of one, delivered as if unanimous, and with the silent acquiescence of lazy or timid associates, by a crafty chief judge, who sophisticates the law to his own mind.

Substantively, Marshall's Court sustained the Federalist vision of rights of contract, property, and national power:

> *I hope that no gentleman will think that state will be called at the bar of a federal court.—John Marshall, June, 1788*

1810: *Fletcher v. Peck.* U.S. Supreme Court asserts the right to invalidate state laws.

1816: *Martin v. Hunter's Lessee.* U.S. Supreme Court asserts the right to invalidate State Supreme Court decisions (Virginia had attempted to confiscate Loyalist properties in violation of national treaties with Great Britain).

1819: *Dartmouth College v. Woodward.* U.S. Supreme Court invalidates the State of New Hampshire's attempts to alter the Charter granted to Dartmouth in 1769 by King George III, on the basis of the contracts clause. (the fact that a Republican legislature was trying to take over a Federalist dominated Board of Trustees had, of course, nothing to do with the outcome of this case).

1823: *McCulloch v. Maryland.* U.S. Supreme Court prevents Maryland from taxing the U.S. Bank, and upholds Hamilton's broad interpretation of the Constitution by sustaining the constitutionality of the National Bank.

1823: *Johnson v. M'Intosh.* The authority of the national government to dispose of Indian lands is upheld. In his decision, Marshall wrote: "Conquest gives a title which the Courts of the conqueror cannot deny, whatever the private or speculative opinions of individuals may be, respecting the original justice of the claim which has been successfully asserted... The title by conquest is acquired and maintained by force. The conqueror prescribes its limits..."

> *Political power issues from the mouth of a gun. —Mao Zedong*

1824: *Gibbons v. Ogden.* Supreme Court sustains Congress' power to regulate interstate commerce (Aaron Ogden had a monopoly to navigate the Hudson granted by New York, and this conflicted with a federal navigating license granted Thomas Gibbons).

ALTERNATIVES TO MARBURY

While Marshall was setting the terms of constitutional debate in years to come, other parties continued asserting their rights to deal with constitutional interpretation.

For example, Jefferson ignored Marshall when Marshall demanded documents from Jefferson for the Aaron Burr treason trial, citing the basis of separation of powers between executive and judiciary. Jefferson wanted Burr convicted, and Marshall responded by giving a narrow construction to the word "treason" which let Burr go free.

IN 1807 PRESIDENT JEFFERSON TRIED TO IGNORE ARTICLE 3 AND HAVE ME TRIED FOR TREASON THE SUPREME COURT STOPPED IT.

TREASON MUST BE ADMITTED IN OPEN COURT OR PROVEN BY TWO WITNESSES.

Aaron Burr

As they served the country in various political offices, both Jefferson and Madison continued to insist on the rights of other parties to interpret the Constitution.

> *You seem to think it devolved on the judges to decide the validity of the*
> *sedition law. But nothing in the Constitution has given them a right to*
> *decide for the Executive, more than to the Executive to decide for them...*
> *the co-ordinate branches [of government] should be checks on each other.*
> *—Thomas Jefferson, Letter to Abigail Adams, Sept. 11, 1804*

> *However true, therefore, it may be, that the judicial*
> *department is, in all questions submitted to it by the*
> *forms of the Constitution, to decide in the last resort, this*
> *resort must necessarily be deemed the last in relation to*
> *the authorities of the other departments of the*
> *government; not in relation to the rights of the parties to*
> *the constitutional compact, from which the judicial as well*
> *as the other departments, hold their delegated trusts.*
> *—James Madison, Report on Virginia Resolutions, 1800*

The New England states took a leaf from the books of Virginia and Kentucky when, in 1814-1815, they met in Hartford, and declared that they should "adopt all such measures as may be necessary effectually to protect the citizens of said states from the operation and effects of all acts which have been or may be passed by the Congress of the United States... not authorized by the Constitution of the United States."

JACKSON

Some of the greatest controversies over who had what to say over the U.S. Constitution occurred during the Presidency of Andrew Jackson (1829-1837).

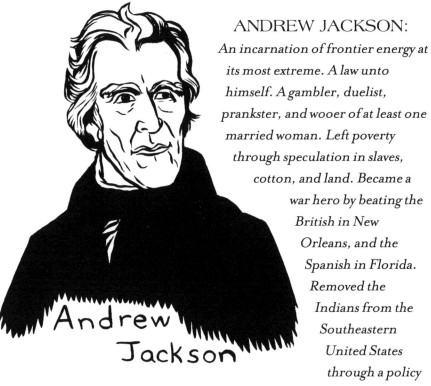

ANDREW JACKSON:

An incarnation of frontier energy at its most extreme. A law unto himself. A gambler, duelist, prankster, and wooer of at least one married woman. Left poverty through speculation in slaves, cotton, and land. Became a war hero by beating the British in New Orleans, and the Spanish in Florida. Removed the Indians from the Southeastern United States through a policy of fraud and violence that presaged 20th century genocide. Now sits on the $20 bill.

Jackson was quite clear about his independent role as an expositor of the Constitution.

> *The opinion of the judges has no more authority over Congress than the opinion of Congress has over the judges, and on that point the President is independent over both. –Andrew Jackson*

"THE OPINION OF THE JUDGES HAS NO MORE AUTHORITY OVER CONGRESS THAN THE OPINION OF CONGRESS HAS OVER THE JUDGES, AND ON THAT POINT THE PRESIDENT IS INDEPENDENT OVER BOTH."
ANDREW JACKSON

Jackson quickly put theory into practice. When a second U.S. Bank Bill was passed and justified on the basis of *McCulloch v. Maryland,* Jackson vetoed it anyway. When South Carolina claimed the right to nullify tariff legislation (borrowing a leaf from the books of Virginia, Kentucky, Connecticut, Massachusetts, Rhode Island, Vermont, and New Hampshire), Jackson threatened to invade South Carolina with an army. When the Marshall Court invalidated a Georgia statute passed in line with Jackson's Indian removal policy, Jackson is said to have remarked, "John Marshall has made his decision, now let him enforce it." When South Carolina cited Georgia's rejection of national authority, Jackson changed his mind. He pushed the litigants to settle, and so organized a united front against South Carolina.

JUDICIAL RETREAT

Though he rejected nullification doctrines, Jackson was more a states' righter than he was a centralizing Federalist. For example, when South Carolina "nullified" a Supreme Court decision validating the rights of freed Negro seamen in Charleston, he did not threaten with another invasion. His policies enjoyed sufficient ratification at the polls that even John Marshall had to take notice. During Marshall's last years on the bench, the court began to accord greater deference to the power of the individual states.

A year after Jackson's election, the right of the states to have some say in commerce was affirmed in *Wilson v. Black Bird Creek March Company* (The *Gibbons v. Ogden* case had been ambivalent on this point).

In *Barrons v. Baltimore* (1832), the Bill of Rights was held to have no application to the state governments. This allowed the states to ignore at least some of the Constitution.

Marshall was succeeded by Jackson's Attorney General, Roger B. Taney.

AFTER MUCH OPPOSITION I WAS ABLE TO HAVE MY FRIEND ROGER TANEY APPOINTED TO BE CHIEF JUSTICE OF THE COURT IN 1836.

THANKS BUDDY.

ROGER TANEY

Maryland hack, Jackson henchman. As provisional Secretary of the Treasury, he helped destroy the second Bank of the United States by withdrawing its government funds. In response, the Senate refused to confirm him as Treasurer. Jackson later rewarded Taney for his loyalty by forcing the Senate to take him as Supreme Court Chief Justice.

Under Taney, the Court took further steps to sanction state powers. *Briscoe v. Bank of Kentucky* (1837) all but erased Marshall's *Craig v. Missouri* (1830), which had disallowed a state from issuing notes of credit.

Perhaps the most controversial decision was *Charles River Bridge v. Warren Bridge Co.* (1837). Massachusetts had granted a group of investors a charter to build a second bridge over the Charles River, which would have put them in competition with an older bridge company with an earlier charter. Federalist Justice Joseph Story said Massachusetts had violated its contract with the earlier group. Jacksonian Justice Roger Taney (with the majority) said Massachusetts could take these measures to promote economic progress. The fact that Federalists (and Whigs) had an old-money constituency and the Jacksonians had a new-money constituency had, of course, nothing to do with the outcome of this case.

TRANSITION

Some of the biggest battles in these years were fought not over people's rights, but states' rights. In general, the people felt better about having political power closer to home, although in many cases these "states' rights" arguments reflected conflicts between local and national elites. While some of the Taney Court's decisions were met with protests when they were initially issued, the controversy did not last. In general, the nation supported a mixture of national and local political power. Moreover, decisions from the Taney court tended to encourage economic initiative on a number of fronts, and Americans have seldom opposed that. For example, *Bank of Augusta v. Earle* (1839) allowed corporations to go national, and *Swift v. Tyson* (1842) helped to establish a national commercial law.

Politics and economy also brought on the next significant constitutional crisis and that was...

SLAVERY!

WARRING OVER THE CONSTITUTION

SLAVERY

Slavery had made problems for the United States that every party had tried to solve. Congress tried to solve them by passing various statutes. Southern states, like South Carolina, thought they could solve them by advocating doctrines like NULLIFICATION, which asserted that a state could invalidate Congress' laws if the state thought they were unconstitutional. For their parts, free states like California, Ohio, and Wisconsin thought they could resist slavery by ignoring slavery enforcement laws that they didn't like. Slaves like Nat Turner and visionaries like John Brown tried to solve the problem through revolt. Abraham Lincoln thought he could help by denying the legitimacy of the war on Mexico.

NAT TURNER: SLAVERY CONTINUED TO BE A PROBLEM. SOME STATES WANTED ABOLITION OTHERS WOULD NOT ALLOW IT.

JOHN BROWN: WE USED REVOLT TO INCITE ABOLITION.

> ...taking for true all the President [Polk] states as facts, he falls short of proving his justification ...I propose to try to show, that the whole of this —issue and evidence—is, from the beginning to end, the sheerest deception... I more than suspect already, that [Polk] is deeply conscious of being in the wrong—that he feels the blood of this war, like the blood of Abel, is crying to Heaven against him. That originally having some strong motive... to involve the two countries in a war, and trusting to escape scrutiny, by fixing the public gaze upon the exceeding brightness of military glory—that attractive rainbow, that rises in showers of blood—that serpent's eye, that charms to destroy—he plunged into it, and has swept on and on, till...he now finds himself, he knows not where. How like the half insane mumblings of a fever-dream, is the whole war part of his late message!
> —Abraham Lincoln, Speech in the U.S. House of Representatives, on Mexican War, January 12, 1848

Stephen Douglas thought he could solve the problem in the territories with local elections. Henry David Thoreau came closer to the solution when he said it was up to the American people.

> *The authority of government, even such as I am willing to submit to… is still an impure one: to be strictly just, it must have the sanction and consent of the governed. It can have no pure right over my person and property but what I concede to it…*
> *—Henry David Thoreau, CIVIL DISOBEDIENCE (1849)*

Then there was Dred Scott...

DRED SCOTT

Dred Scott had been a slave who had spent time in free territory before he was taken back into the slave holding state of Missouri. Scott's owners, the President of the United States, and the Justices of the Supreme Court decided that through his situation the Supreme Court might solve the problem of slavery. Scott's Missouri master sent ownership papers to his brother-in-law in New York to ensure that a federal court could hear the case. When President Buchanan (1857-1861) heard that the Supreme Court members were discussing a narrowly based decision, he encouraged them instead to render a broad-ranging opinion.

Some Justices agreed, and 6 of them (5 of them southerners) decided that not only could Scott not sue because he was not a citizen, they also decided that the Constitution said that Congress could not regulate slavery in U.S. territories:

In the opinion of the court, the legislation and histories of the times, and the language used in the Declaration of Independence, show, that neither the class of persons who had been imported as slaves, nor their descendants, whether they had become free or not, were then acknowledged as a part of the people, nor intended to be included in the general words used in that memorable instrument. ...

They had for more than a century before been regarded as beings of an inferior order, and altogether unfit to associate with the white race, either in social or political relations; and so far inferior, that they had no rights which the white man was bound to respect; and that the negro might justly and lawfully be reduced to slavery for his benefit. He was bought and sold, and treated as an ordinary article of merchandise and traffic, whenever a profit could be made by it. This opinion was at that time fixed and universal in the civilized portion of the white race....

The *Dred Scott* decision upset a number of Americans.

...if the policy of the Government upon vital questions affecting the whole people is to be irrevocably fixed by decisions of the Supreme Court... the people will have ceased to be their own rulers... —Abraham Lincoln

WAR ISSUES

The nation had depended upon Congress to juggle a balance between slave and free states. The *Dred Scott* decision undercut Congress' ability to juggle any longer.

When Lincoln was elected President (1860), one last-minute compromise proposal was offered in Congress, which would have created a 13th amendment to the Constitution guaranteeing slavery in the Southern states (but not in the territories). This measure failed.

ABRAHAM LINCOLN:

From backwoods rube to corporate lawyer. Under a homespun exterior operated one of the shrewdest political minds the nation has witnessed. According to his law partner, "his ambition was a little engine that knew no rest." Master of English prose with the vision of a tragic poet. Seldom has anyone expressed so much profundity with so few words: "as Labor is the common BURTHEN ... so the effort of SOME to shift their share of the burthen on to the shoulders of OTHERS, is the great, durable curse of the [human] race."

The Southern states seceded, many of them through dubiously organized conventions. The arguments they used asserted that the Constitution was a compact between sovereign states; since the Northern states' approach to slavery violated this compact, the Southern states had a right to leave.

For his part, Lincoln maintained that the Constitution was a compact of the sovereign people:

This country, with its institutions, belongs to the people who inhabit it. Whenever they shall grow weary of the existing government, they can exercise their constitutional right of amending it or their revolutionary right to dismember or overthrow it... Why should there not be a patient confidence in the ultimate justice of the people? (March 4, 1861)

WAR

Jefferson Davis, President of the Confederacy, expressed the Southern point of view:

Jefferson Davis

This was one argument the Supreme Court could not resolve.

An organization created by the States... has been gradually perverted into a machine for their control in their domestic affairs. The creature has been exalted above its creators; the principals have been made subordinate to the agent appointed by themselves... so utterly have the principles of the Constitution been corrupted in the Northern mind that, in the inaugural address delivered by President Lincoln in March last, he asserts as an axiom, which he plainly deems to be undeniable, that the theory of all the Constitution requires that in all cases the majority shall govern... This is the lamentable and fundamental error on which rests the policy that has culminated in his declaration of war against these Confederate States...
(April 29, 1861)

RESOLUTION

Lincoln understood it as a fight for democracy, and said so:

Abraham Lincoln

> *Our popular government has often been called an experiment. Two points in it, our people have already settled—the successful establishing and the successful administering of it. One still remains—its successful maintenance against a formidable internal attempt to overthrow it. It is now for them to demonstrate to the world that those who can fairly carry an election can also suppress a rebellion... Such will be a great lesson of peace; teaching men that what they cannot take by an election, neither can they take it by a war; teaching all the folly of being the beginners of a war.*
> —Abraham Lincoln, July 4, 1861

Many others agreed:

> *If monarchy would be better, it might be wise to quite fighting, admit that a Republic is too weak to take care of itself, and invite some deposed Duke or Prince of Europe to come over here and rule us.*
> —Indianapolis newspaper

> *[If this modern free government fails] ... the old cry will be sent forth from the aristocrats of Europe that such is the common lot of all republics...*
> —Irish immigrant, Union soldier

> *I believe that the dissolution of the Union is inevitable, and that men before me will live to see an aristocracy established in America.*
> —Earl of Shrewsbury

...we all expect, we nearly all wish, success to the Confederate cause.
—TIMES of London

...the work of George Washington has come to an end...
—LA PATRIE, French newspaper

...the great body of the aristocracy and the commercial classes are anxious to see the United States go to pieces.
—Charles Francis Adams, U.S. Ambassador to Britain

The republican form of government ... is breaking down ... What can be expected from a country where men of humble origin are elevated to the highest position? This is democracy in practice, the democracy that European theorists rave about....
—Russia's ambassador to U.S.

After 600,000 deaths, Lincoln's side won.

EMANCIPATION

13thAmendment

PROHIBITION OF SLAVERY

After the Civil War, the problem of slavery seemed solved. The Southern states were *told* to ratify a THIRTEENTH AMENDMENT different from the one offered 5 years earlier, and in December of 1865, the Constitution had a new provision abolishing slavery:

> *Neither slavery nor involuntary servitude, except as punishment for crime whereof the party shall have been convicted, shall exist within the United States or any place subject to their jurisdiction...*

(Lincoln's famous EMANCIPATION PROCAMATION had freed slaves only in territory held by Confederate troops.)

RECONSTRUCTION

However, if the problems of slavery were resolved, the problems of racism were not. Neither were questions of constitutional balance.

WHEN PRESIDENT LINCOLN WAS ASSASSINATED IT WAS UP TO ME TO TRY TO BRING BACK SOUTHERN STATES BACK AND UPHOLD THE 13th AMENDMENT.

Andrew Johnson

In 1865, Lincoln had a plan for "reconstructing" the Southern states, and bringing them back into the Union. However, he was assassinated by a Southern sympathizer. Lincoln's successor, Andrew Johnson, attempted to implement Lincoln's program. It backfired. Southern states sent ex-Confederate military commanders to Congress, including a Confederate Vice President. They passed "black codes," which made black people into something more than slaves, but something less than real citizens.

> All penal and criminal laws now in force describing the mode of punishment of crimes and misdemeanors committed by slaves, free negroes, or mulattoes are hereby re-enacted, and decreed to be in full force against all freedmen, free negroes and mulattoes.
> —MISSISSIPPI PENAL CODE

Northern congressmen were outraged. They threw the representatives from the Southern states out of Congress and passed measures designed to aid and protect blacks. When President Johnson resisted a number of these measures, the battle lines were drawn. The election of 1866 sent overwhelming majorities to Congress supporting the "radicals."

IMPEACHING JOHNSON

With the new majorities, the "radical" Congress implemented its own version of "RECONSTRUCTION." It put the Southern states under military rule. Under the leadership of Representative Thad Stevens and Charles Sumner, it passed a number of civil rights acts, the constitutionality of which it ensured by passing the 14th and 15th AMENDMENTS to the Constitution.

XIV. All persons born or naturalized in the United States, and subject to the jurisdiction thereof, are citizens of the United States and of the State wherein they reside. No State shall make or enforce any law which shall abridge the privileges or immunities of citizens of the United States; nor shall any State deprive any person of life, liberty, or property, without due process of law; nor deny to any person within its jurisdiction the equal protection of the laws.

THE 14th AMENDMENT CREATED A NEW DEFINITION OF CITIZENSHIP. STATES MUST OBSERVE THE RIGHTS OF ALL U.S. CITIZENS.

Thaddeus Stevens

14th Amendment

> *XV. The right of citizens of the United States to vote shall not be denied or abridged by the United States or by any State on account of race, color, or previous condition of servitude.*

When Johnson attempted to resist this, the House of Representatives voted to impeach him. However, the Senate failed to convict him by one vote. Though Johnson had resisted laws passed by Congress, he was found not guilty of "high crimes and misdemeanors."

SUPREME
COURT
TAP-DANCES

During these tumultuous years, the Supreme Court did more tap-dancing over what was "really" constitutional than Congress ever had to do over slavery. In periods of intense political struggle, the law's supposed stability frequently gives way to expediency.

In 1861, pro-confederate mobs in Baltimore attacked union troops. Lincoln declared martial law. John Merryman recruited and trained rebel soldiers, and worked to cut telegraph wires and destroy bridges. Union troops arrested him for treason and refused to release him so he could show up in court. The right to have reasons for jailing a person had been taken from the Glorious Revolution of 1688 and put into Article I, Section 9, of the Constitution:

> The Privilege of the Writ of Habeas Corpus shall not be suspended, unless when in Cases of Rebellion or Invasion the public Safety may require it.

Merryman's lawyers complained to Chief Justice Taney who was happy to tell Lincoln he could not suspend habeas corpus (*Ex Parte Merryman*). Lincoln told Taney that he was sorry, but he was busy fighting a civil war:

> *Thoroughly imbued with a reverence for the guaranteed rights of individuals, I was slow to adopt the strong measures which, by degrees, I have been forced to regard as being within the exceptions of the Constitution and indispensable to the public safety... I concede that the class of arrests complained of can be constitutional only when in cases of rebellion or invasion the public safety may require them.*

So in 1863, the Supreme Court refused to hear a case involving the holding of a civilian by a military court (*Ex Parte Vallandigham*, 1864). After the war, however, the Court would reverse a case of a civilian convicted by a military court (*Ex Parte Milligan* , 1866).

During the war, the Court refused to hear a case challenging the government's authority to issue paper money (*Roosevelt v. Meyer*, 1863). In *Hepburn v. Griswold* (1870), however, it held that a creditor could refuse paper money as payment for debt. Within 15 months, President Grant (elected in 1868) appointed two new Justices, and the *Hepburn* case was reversed.

After the war, the nation's efforts to rebuild came to be called Reconstruction. On the one hand, the Court protected some ex-Confederate officers with the ex post facto clause, which prohibits criminalizing an act which was legal when it was performed (*Cummings v. Missouri* [1867], *Ex Parte Garland* [1867]). On the other hand, when Congress imposed military rule over the Southern states, it denied the Supreme Court jurisdiction to review the habeas corpus act it passed in conjunction with that legislation. In general, the Supreme Court sustained Congress' Reconstruction laws (*Mississippi v. Johnson* [1867], *Georgia v. Stanton* [1867], *ExParte McCardle* [1869], *Texas v. White* [1869]).

SUPREME COURT GUTS THE 14TH AMENDMENT

Originally, the 14th Amendment was passed to force state governments to respect human rights, just like the Bill of Rights forced the federal government to respect human rights (Recall that in *Barron v. Baltimore*, John Marshall said the Bill of Rights did not apply to the states). What the state governments did in the 19th century was very important to individual citizens, because they frequently exercised more power over everybody's day-to-day affairs than did the federal government.

But whatever the American people wanted from the 14th Amendment when they ratified it in 1868, in 1873, the Court refused to use it to overrule *Barron v. Baltimore* and hold the states accountable to a broad list of individual rights. Louisiana had granted one group of butchers a monopoly to pursue their trade. In the *Slaughterhouse Cases* (1873), the Court told the butchers left out in the cold that the 14th Amendment protected only federally secured rights, not state-secured rights.

This gutting of the 14th Amendment was also used to sustain state statutes which prohibited women from voting (*Minor v. Happersett*, 1875) and engaging in the practice of law:

> ...*in view of the peculiar characteristics, destiny and mission of women, it is within the province of the Legislature to ordain what offices, positions, and callings shall be filled and discharged by men... —Bradwell v. Illinois, 1873*

Though the 14th Amendment was undercut for the sake of state governments in the cases of women and blacks, in a few years it would be used liberally against state governments for the sake of the wealthy.

YEARS OF REACTION

THE COMPROMISE OF 1877

The Civil War's constitutional issues, which had centered on human rights, climaxed and faded with the presidential election of 1876. When the returns came in, Democrat Samuel J. Tilden had 184 certain electoral votes, and Republican Rutherford B. Hayes had only 165. However, 185 votes were needed to win and 20 electoral votes remained contested and uncounted. There were questions as to whether this election would have to be settled like the one 16 years before—that is, by military force.

Rutherford Hayes

In January 1877, Congress appointed a commission to investigate these issues and make recommendations to Congress. In February, northern Republicans and southern Democrats cut a deal (later known as the COMPROMISE OF 1877). It was supposed to include the following terms:

1. Republican Hayes would become President.

2. Hayes would end the army's occupation of the South;

3. Hayes would give the Democrats a cabinet post replete with patronage opportunities;

4. Hayes would support capital improvements in the South;

5. Hayes would support a southern transcontinental railroad.

6. Southern Democrats would accept the spirit of Reconstruction;

7. Republican James Garfield would be elected Speaker of the House.

The commission duly "elected" Hayes when 8 Republicans out-voted 7 Democrats on the matter of allocating the disputed electoral votes. Congress accepted the findings on March 2, and on March 5, Hayes was inaugurated President. Hayes implemented terms (2) and (3) of the Compromise. And then, like other deals in American political history including the broken promise to John Hancock which was to give him a Vice Presidency for his cooperation, it fell apart. But here, the big losers were southern Blacks.

What the Compromise of 1877 salvaged in terms of political quietude, it lost in terms of principled decency. Concern for human rights was giving way to racism and greed.

THE LAWYERS TAKE OVER

At bottom the Compromise politicians were doing only what the rest of the country was doing, viz., grabbing at everything. These were the days of the Gilded Age, when Robber Barons used corporations to produce profits by any means necessary, including bribery, monopoly, and guns.

The order of the day was avarice, and to protect this order, various ideologues justified it with words like "personal liberty," "freedom," "nature," "individualism," "survival of the fittest," and so on.

Lawyers (and judges) representing the very rich banded together in conferences and organizations to encourage one another to use these words to translate the Constitution. Indeed, they began to assert that interpreting the Constitution was such a specialized science that only they could do it. The result was a string of Supreme Court decisions designed to suppress anyone who got in the way of the free, white and wealthy.

1875: Supreme Court Justice Samuel Miller: "It is vain to contend with Judges who have been at the bar the advocates for forty years of railroad companies, and all forms of associated capital."

1877: Railroad strike around the country; general strike in St. Louis. Hayes calls out federal troops to squish all strikers.

1878: American Bar Association formed.

1879: ABA President Phelps tries to use professionalism to squelch democracy: "...it is too true the [the Constitution] has become more and more a subject to be hawked about the country," by those "who have never found leisure for the graces of English grammar."

1883: U.S. Supreme Court holds that Reconstruction Act (designed to protect blacks) does *not* apply to Ku Klux Klan terrorism or white discrimination in the absence of state action (*States v. Harris, Civil Rights Cases*).

Mere discrimination on account of race or color was not regarded as a badge of slavery.
—Joseph P. Bradley, for majority:

I cannot resist the conclusion that the substance and spirit of the recent [14th] amendment to the Constitution have been sacrificed by a subtle and ingenious verbal criticism.
—John Marshall Harlan, dissent:

1886: Corporation recognized as a "person" enjoying all the rights that human persons enjoy. *Santa Clara County v. Southern Pacific Railroad Company.* During this year, the Court invalidates 230 state laws designed to regulate corporations.

1892: Homestead Strike in Pennsylvania; state calls out militia to squish strikers. General Strike in New Orleans; state calls out militia to squish strikers. Populists adopt OMAHA PLATFORM, calling for popular control of the currency, support for the Knights of Labor, a graduated income tax, nationalization of the railroads, eight hour work day, and popular election of Senators.

1893: Supreme Court Justice David Brewer addresses New York State Bar Association: "It is the unvarying law that the wealth of the community will be in the hands of the few..."

1894: Pullman Strike. Led by future socialist Eugene Debs, railroad workers stop Midwestern railroad traffic. President Cleveland calls out federal troops to squish strikers.

1895: Ignoring years of precedent, *Pollock v. Farmers Loan and Trust Co.* responds to corporate lawyer Joseph Choate's appeal to halt the "communist march," and holds income tax laws unconstitutional. Basically, the government is forbidden to force the rich to pay a fair share of society's expenses.

— *U.S. v. E. K. Knight Co.* holds that a sugar trust manufacturing 90% of the nation's sugar does NOT violate the SHERMAN ANTI-TRUST ACT because such involves local manufacture and not interstate commerce (the Sherman Anti-Trust Act had been passed to curtail monopoly in American business, although after *Knight* it was hard to tell WHAT the Supreme Court would consider a monopoly).

— In *In re Debs*, the Supreme Court did find one use for the Sherman Anti-Trust Act: union busting. It held that the Act could be used to control union activity during a strike.

— A New York banker toasted the Supreme Court: "I give you, gentlemen, the Supreme Court of the United States—guardian of the dollar, defender of private property, enemy of spoliation, sheet anchor of the Republic."

1896: The Supreme Court sanctions Louisiana segregation laws in *Plessy v. Ferguson.*

> *If one race be inferior to the other socially, the*
> *Constitution of the United States cannot put them upon*
> *the same plane... —Henry Billings Brown, for the majority*

> *The destinies of the two races, in this country, are*
> *indissolubly linked together, and the interests of both*
> *require that the common government of all shall not*
> *permit the seeds of race hate to be planted under the*
> *sanction of the law. —Harlan, dissent*

1897: In *Davis v. Massachusetts,* the Supreme Court upholds the conviction of William Davis for preaching on the Boston Common without a permit:

> *For the legislature absolutely or conditionally to forbid public*
> *speaking in a highway or public park is no more an infringement*
> *on the rights of a member of the public than for the owner of a*
> *private house to forbid it in his house. —Oliver Wendell Holmes*

1905: The Supreme Court invalidates state legislation limiting bakers' working hours to 60 per week in *Lochner v. New York.*

1908: Supreme Court invalidates legislation making it a crime for an employer to fire an employee because of union membership (Adair v. U.S.), and awards treble damages against a union for a secondary boycott under the Sherman Anti-Trust Act (Loewe v. Lawlor).

THE PEOPLE FIGHT BACK

The number of statutes that the Supreme Court invalidated indicates that the people were not idle in trying to protect themselves. Between 1876 and 1896 much of the story involves growing consciousness and coordination between southern farmers and northern workers, blacks, whites and women, who have collectively been called Populists. In 1892 their People's Party's adopted the Omaha Platform.

> *From the same prolific womb of governmental injustice we breed the two great classes—tramps and millionaires... We believe that the powers of government—in other words, of the people—should be expanded ... as rapidly and as far as the good sense of an intelligent people and the teachings of experience shall justify, to the end that oppression, injustice, and poverty shall eventually cease in the land. —People's Party Omaha Platform, July 4, 1892*

The election of 1896 saw the co-optation and smashing of this movement. Democrats advocated silver based money (instead of Republican gold or Populist paper). Terrorists hung men from trees and whipped women with barbed wire. When election officers found ballots they didn't like they tossed them out. To bolster their terror and fraud, the Bourbons (rich whites) in southern states resorted to legal "reform." To discourage minority and lower class voting, they enacted poll taxes, literacy tests, and burdensome voter registration requirements. To discourage the development of third parties, they outlawed "fusion" voting. ("Fusion" voting allows minor parties to take some major party candidates onto their ballot lines, thus drawing attention to their candidates on other ballot lines who have not been approved by the major parties—usually because they are too "radical.")

What remained were middle class reformers who have been called Progressives. In 1913, they finally forced Congress and the legislatures to pass two amendments to the Constitution, theoretically beyond the bite of the Supreme Court (although we have already seen what the Supreme Court managed to do with the Fourteenth Amendment).

The SIXTEENTH AMENDMENT was designed to overrule *Pollack v. Farmers Loan and Trust Co.*, give power to the government, and force the rich to give some of their wealth back to society:

16th Amendment

XVI: The Congress shall have power to lay and collect taxes on incomes, from whatever source derived, without apportionment among the several States, and without regard to any census or enumeration.

The SEVENTEENTH AMENDMENT gave the people the right to elect their own Senators. Heretofore, Senators had been elected by state legislatures (It's a lot easier to buy one state legislature than it is to buy the whole state).

SENATORS WILL BE ELECTED BY THE PEOPLE.

VOTE ✓

17th Amendment 1913

XVII: The Senate of the United States shall be composed of two Senators from each State, elected by the people thereof...

Corporate corruption would be addressed, as long as it did not involve democratic control of the money supply, mobilization of farmers and workers, and co-operation between whites and blacks. By the turn of the century, even Theodore Roosevelt could advocate reform.

> Every man holds his property subject to the general right of the community to regulate its use to whatever degree the public welfare may require it. —Theodore Roosevelt, 1910

Yet whatever additional hopes that Progressivism might have held for the nation were soon wiped out by...

WORLD WAR I

President Wilson knew what would happen if he led the nation into war:

WORLD WAR ONE WOULD HAVE A MAJOR IMPACT ON HOW THE CONSTITUTION WOULD BE INTERPRETED.

Once lead this people into war, and they'll forget there ever was such a thing as tolerance. To fight you must be brutal and ruthless, and the spirit of ruthless brutality will enter into the very fibre of our national life, infecting Congress, the court, the policeman on the beat, the man in the street...

WOODROW WILSON

In spite of the fact that the British violated American neutrality rights as much as the Germans, Wilson used the latter's unrestricted warfare as a means of leading the nation into war. His decision, of course, had nothing to do with the fact that Americans financiers had loaned the Allies more than $2 billion, as opposed to a mere $27 million to the Germans...

DEMOCRACY AT HOME KILLED TO "SAVE DEMOCRACY" ABROAD

Wilson was quite right about what would happen to America, should it go to war. With his Espionage Act (1917) and Sedition Act (1918), Wilson surpassed the Alien and Sedition Act of 1798 in both quantity and quality:

> QUANTITY
> — 1798 and after: 25 prosecutions, 10 convictions
> — 1917 and after: more than 1500 prosecutions, more than 1000 convictions

QUALITY
- Socialist Congressman Berger gets 20 years for calling war a capitalist conspiracy;
- Socialist Presidential candidate Eugene Debs gets 20 years for statements having a "tendency" to encourage draft resistance;
- Over 100 Chicago IWW members convicted for opposing war effort;
- Film producer sentenced to 10 years for film celebrating American Revolution because of its implied criticism of the British;
- Farmer gets 21 months for comparing Germans in Belgium to Americans in Philippines.

We must purify the sources of America's population and keep it pure ... I am myself an American and I love to preach my doctrine before 100 percent Americans, because my platform is 100% Americanism. –Attorney General Mitchell Palmer

The Supreme Court held these acts constitutional as soon as it was able (*Schencks v. U.S. Abrams v. U.S.,* [1919]).

The war encouraged repression in America and revolution in Russia, which in turn encouraged even more repression in America. In 1919, strikes were broken across the country. Whites killed blacks in some 25 different race riots. Under Attorney General A. Mitchell Palmer, over 200 persons were deported to Russia without a hearing. Thousands of homes and offices were raided In New York, 5 duly elected Socialist officials were expelled from the state legislature. J. Edgar Hoover got his start heading the new General Intelligence division, keeping files on various radicals.

19th Amendment

MORE AMENDMENTS

Immediately after World War I, the Constitution was amended twice.

With a million-dollar grant from a woman's magazine publisher, coupled with conscientious organizing, women finally secured the right to vote with the NINE-TEENTH AMENDMENT:

> *The right of citizens of the United States to vote shall not be denied or abridged by the United States or by any State on account of sex.*

This victory for an elementary democratic right did not come without controversy. Some thought the vote for women would help protect the country from riff raff, immigrants, and Negroes:

...this government is menaced with great danger. That danger lies in the slums of the cities, and the ignorant foreign vote. ... There is but one way to avert the danger... cut off the vote of the slums and give it to women... the usefulness of woman suffrage [is] a counterbalance to the foreign vote, and is a means of legally preserving white supremacy in the South...
—Carrie Chapman Catt, Suffragist Leader

For others, the right seemed marginal, given how capital dominated political processes and economic conditions:

> *Our democracy is but a name. We vote? What does that mean? It means that we choose between two bodies of real, though not avowed, autocrats. We choose between Tweedledum and Tweedledee.* —Helen Keller

> *Our modern fetish is universal suffrage. The women of Australia and New Zealand can vote, and help make the laws. Are the labor conditions better there?* —Emma Goldman

In the meantime, PROHIBITION ascended to constitutional status, having been elevated in a war-atmosphere which

- Emphasized eating grain instead of drinking it
- Hated Germans and their occupations (like brewing)
- Demanded conformity

(That saloons frequently served as meeting places for labor union and urban ward bosses mobilizing the "foreign" vote had nothing, of course, to do with the passage of this amendment).

Laws passed under Prohibition's Eighteenth Amendment were consistently violated until 1933, when two new amendments were added to the Constitution. The Twenty-first Amendment abolished prohibition, and the Twentieth adjusted some dates for terms of office: the President now starts his or her term in January; it used to be March.

SUPREME COURT
BACKS REACTION

In the meantime, the Supreme Court continued to promote the status quo that Americans had begun to know, if not love.

It invalidated laws that attempted to regulate child labor: *Hammer v. Dagenhart* (1918), *Bailey v. Drexel Furniture* (1922).

It took the Sherman Act, which Congress had passed to control monopolistic corporations, and applied it to labor unions—and any damages found against the unions would be tripled: *UMW v. Coronado Coal Co.* (1922).

It held that courts might issue injunctions if unions picketed; attempted to organize employees who had signed non-union contracts; or engaged in secondary boycotts: *American Steel Foundries v. Tri-City Central Trades Council* (1921), *Truax v. Corrigan* (1921), *Hitchman Coal and Coke Co. v. Mitchell* (1917), *Duplex Printing Press Co. v. Deergin* (1921), *Bedford Cut Stone Company v. Journeymen Stone Cutters Association* (1927).

Between 1880 and 1930, the injunction was used 1845 times against labor, 921 times during 1920-1930.

> *Since 1920, the Court has invalidated more legislation than in fifty years preceding. Views that were antiquated twenty-five years ago have been resurrected in decisions nullifying:*
>
> — *minimum wage laws for women in industry,*
>
> — *a standard-weight bread law to protect bakers from short weights and honest bakers from unfair competition,*
>
> — *a law fixing the resale price of theatre tickets by ticket scalpers in New York,*
>
> — *laws controlling exploitation of the unemployed by employment agencies,*
>
> — *and many tax laws...*
>
> *Merely as a matter or arithmetic, this is an impressive mortality rate.*
> —*Felix Frankfurter, Future Supreme Court Justice, 1930*

> *The Dogberries of the Federal bench, as usual, lend themselves willingly to the buffoonery: dozens of injunctions issue from their mills every day...*
> —*H. L. Mencken*

TAFT AND HUGHES

The court was guided in its course by the steady right hand of former President William Howard Taft.

WILLIAM HOWARD TAFT

Bloated in body and soul, Taft serves the interests of his class with a conscientiousness that is matched only by its viciousness. During the Pullman strike, Taft reads that federal troops killed thirty strikers. To a friend he writes: "Everybody hopes that it is true."

William Howard Taft

From his seat on the Supreme Court, he observes:

> *The only class which is distinctly arrayed against the Court is a class that does not like the Courts at any rate, and that is organized labor. That faction we have to hit every little while, because they are continually violating the law and depending on threats and violence to accomplish their purpose.*

Taft knew why he took the office of Chief Justice. Shortly after being appointed (1921), he told his fellow justices that he had been chosen "to reverse a few decisions." He also knew why he stayed on the bench:

> *As long as things continue as they are, and I am able to answer in my place, I must stay on the Court in order to prevent the Bosheviki from getting control....*

The Supreme Court's stranglehold on the Constitution seemed secure when Charles Evan Hughes replaced Taft in 1930.

CHARLES EVAN HUGHES:

Justice
Charles
Evans
Hughes

Child prodigy, governor of New York, GOP presidential candidate, Secretary of State, World Court judge, ex-Associate Supreme Court Justice. Scammed out of Chief Supreme Court Justice position in 1910 by Taft, who, while suggesting to Hughes that the post was his, nevertheless appointed another, older man, so that Taft would have a chance to take the seat later (which he did).

No man in public life so exemplifies the influence of powerful combinations in the political and financial world as does Mr. Hughes. —George W. Norris, Populist Senator

We are under a Constitution, but the Constitution is what the judges say it is. —Charles Evan Hughes

THE DEPRESSION

With the stock market crash of 1929, the economy fell into an abyss that traumatized the nation. Between 1929 and 1932, thousands of banks and more than 100,000 businesses failed. Capital investment fell from $10 billion in 1929 to $1 billion in 1932, and unemployment skyrocketed from 4 to 11 million people, some one quarter of the labor force. Industrial production and personal incomes halved.

Many Americans were upset with this situation. They took over buildings, like state capitols and city banks. In the farmland, lawyers and judges who processed mortgage foreclosures were beaten and killed. Working people joined unions, held strikes, took over factories, and halted almost everything in Minneapolis, Toledo, and San Francisco.

YEARS OF REFORM

In the meantime, the Supreme Court continued to invalidate laws establishing railroad pensions, state minimum wage laws, and federal regulations concerning coal and farm production. Many of the Court's reactionary decisions rested on votes of 6-3 or 5-4.

A crisis of constitutional if not revolutionary proportions was brewing.

THE NEW DEAL

In 1932, the country elected a new Congress and a new President (Franklin D. Roosevelt). In 1933, they took office and began searching for legislative solutions to the economic mess. In the words of Huey Long, some programs like the National Industrial Recovery Act had "every fault of socialism... without one of its virtues," presumably because it tried to regulate the economy without redistributing wealth. Other programs, like the Tennessee Valley Authority, showed that public planning could provide much of what private capitalism would or could not: e.g., cheap electric power, flood control, soil conservation, navigable rivers...

This array of attacks on economic disaster was known as FDR's NEW DEAL. The "new" part was the fact that government actually worried about capitalism's awful effects on individual human beings, and sometimes tried to do something to limit those effects. The "deal" part was that capitalism was going to be preserved, whether it deserved it or not.

AMERICA, DO I HAVE A DEAL FOR YOU!

Franklin Delano Roosevelt

For its part, the Supreme Court acted like Roger Taney against Abraham Lincoln, obstructing progress wherever it could. In 1935, it began invalidating major pieces of New Deal legislation. Roosevelt and Congress responded with the "Second New Deal," which established Social Security as well as a system for protecting workers who wanted to organize into unions. (National Labor Relations Act).

But there remained the question of how the Supreme Court would deal with these new attempts to protect people from capitalism's worst excesses.

THE JUDICIAL REVOLUTION OF 1937

For better or worse, the so-called JUDICIAL REVOLUTION OF 1937 resolved the crisis. Part of the story is told by its chronology:

— November, 1936: FDR enjoys landslide victory.

— February 7, 1937: FDR announces his "Court-packing plan." Based on ideas originally proposed by Supreme Court Justice J. C. McReynolds, when he had been attorney general, FDR proposes that he be allowed to appoint additional judges for benches where judges of retirement age are sitting. This would have allowed him to appoint enough new justices to the Supreme Court to outnumber the reactionary majority.

> *We cannot yield our constitutional destiny to the personal judgment of a few men who, being fearful of the future, would deny us the necessary means of dealing with the present... —President FDR*

— March 29, 1937: Hughes and Roberts join 3 progressive Justices to sustain a state minimum-wage law for women in *West Coast Hotel v. Parish*, reversing *Morehead v. Tipaldo* from 1936.

— April 12, 1937: Another 5-4 decision sustains the NATIONAL LABOR RELATIONS ACT.

— May 18, 1937: Eldest of the conservative block of four (Justice Willis Van Devanter) announces that he will retire from the Court on June 1.

— May 24, 1937: Provisions of the SOCIAL SECURITY ACT upheld by votes of 5-4 (*Helvering v. Davis*) and 7-2 (*Steward Machine Co. v. Davis*).

The other part of the story is that the critical swing vote seems to have been ready to shift before FDR announced his court-packing plan. Owen Roberts changed gears in 1937. Judges rarely tip their hands, but in 1951, Roberts gave his explanation as to why he began switching his votes:

> *Looking back, it is difficult to see how the Court could have resisted the popular urge for uniform standards throughout the country—for what in effect was a unified economy...*
>
> *An insistency by the court on holding federal power to what seemed its appropriate orbit when the Constitution was adopted might have resulted in even more radical changes in our dual structure than those which have been gradually accomplished through the extension of the limited jurisdiction on the federal government.*

In other words, either we change our minds to agree with what the people want, or the people will revolt.

THE NEW COURT: CLOSURES

After the "switch in time that saved nine" (as some wags called it), the conservative justices began to retire. Roosevelt replaced them with judges sympathetic to the New Deal. In the end, FDR appointed a total of eight new Justices.

On the one hand, the new court ensured that the most fundamental rights of the rich would be preserved. It reigned in the power of labor where it counted most, viz., at the site of the means of production. In *NLRB v. Fansteel* (1939), the Court declared factory "sit-down" strikes illegal. In a "sit-down," workers would occupy their factory by sitting at their posts, thereby preventing the bosses from sending in scabs (who might take their jobs); or goons (who might damage them—or factory property). For workers, the "sit-down" was both safe and effective. By prohibiting this powerful but non-violent resistance to management violence, *Fansteel* made it clear

that the Supreme Court was more worried about worker (non-violent) illegalities than management (violent) illegalities, and that capitalism was more important to the American order than fairness. Limiting power was fine if you talked about it in terms of constitutional rhetoric, as long as you didn't try to apply it to managerial prerogatives.

STRIKES ARE ILLEGAL HERE.

WORKER RIGHTS

THE NEW COURT: OPENINGS

On the other hand, while the Court did its best to check labor's advances into its most critical arena, it did concede the power to organize to ordinary people in a number of other significant areas. It rendered a number of decisions that constituted important turning points in the development of American civil liberties. From one perspective, these decisions might be seen simply as a means of enhancing the support for the New Deal. From another perspective, they can be viewed as attempts to raise the Constitution to a level of minimal democracy.

The new Court began to re-instate the right to picket in *Senn v. Tile Lawyers Union* (1937) and *Thornhill v. Alabama* (1940).

It opened the way for the Bill of Rights to be applied to the States in *Palko v. Connecticut* (1937).

It overturned *Davis v. Massachusetts* and declared that the parks and streets were the property not of the state, but of the people, in *Hague v. CIO* (1939).

In a number of cases, the Court restricted the right of government to interfere with grassroots leafleting and door-knocking *Lovell v. Griffin (1938), Schneider v. Irvington* (1939), *Cantwell v. Connecticut* (1940), *Martin v. Struthers* (1943).

In the case of a company town, it limited the owning corporation's capacity to restrict the rights of free speech *Marsh v. Alabama* (1946).

One of the most significant cases was *U.S. v. Carolene Products* (1938). Though it dealt with adulterated milk, the decision contained a footnote intimating that the Court was ready to look as rigorously at laws affecting the rights of ordinary people as it had (for the past 50 years) scrutinized the laws that affected the rights of the super-rich. It put litigants on notice that if a law could be viewed as unduly restrictive or discriminatory, the Supreme Court would be more disposed to invalidate it.

Besides the cases already mentioned, in *Smith v. Allwright* (1944), the Court reversed a 1935 decision which had sanctioned all-white primaries.

WAR AGAIN

History suggests that elites stand all too ready to use war to limit individual rights and hinder social progress. Adventures abroad are used to resolve—or avoid—problems at home. One can argue over how well World War II fits this pattern. World War II solved the immediate economic problems of the Depression. Its political legacy was more complicated.

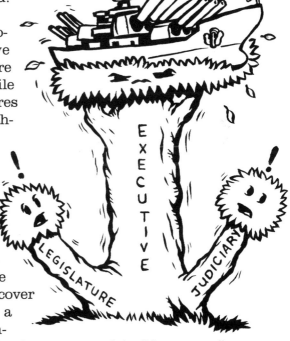

Under President Roosevelt, the executive branch assumed more and more power. While some of these measures helped defeat Hitler, others set precedents with noxious repercussions for years to come. Without congressional authorization, Roosevelt sent ships to Great Britain, and instituted undeclared warfare against Germany. To cover himself, he declared a limited state of national emergency in September 1939 and in May 1941 "unlimited" that state. In 1942 he threatened to "nullify" a provision of legislation (the EMERGENCY PRICE CONTROL ACT) if Congress failed to repeal it:

> *In the event that the Congress should fail to act, and act adequately, I shall accept the responsibility, and I will act. … The American people can be sure that I will use my powers with a full sense of responsibility to the Constitution and to my country. The American people can also be sure that I shall not hesitate to use every power vested in me to accomplish the defeat of our enemies in any part of the world where our own safety demands such defeat. And when the war is won, the powers under which I act will automatically revert to the people of the United States—to the people to whom those powers belong.*

Congress repealed the section.

Some of Roosevelt's actions were particularly problematic, like when he seized a steel mill in order to stop workers from striking; or when he sent thousands of Japanese into detention camps. The Congress belatedly sanctioned the former with the WAR LABOR DISPUTES ACT, and the Supreme Court sanctioned the latter in *Korematsu v. U.S.* (1944).

FDR'S SECOND BILL OF RIGHTS

Was FDR more like Lincoln or Wilson when he fought his war? On January 11, 1944, he broadcast a speech where he proposed that Congress pass a second Bill of Rights for the American people:

This Republic had its beginning, and grew to its present strength, under the protection of certain inalienable political rights—among them the right of free speech, free press, free worship, trial by jury, freedom from unreasonable searches and seizures. They were our rights to life and liberty.

As our Nation has grown in size and stature, however—as our industrial economy expanded—these political rights proved inadequate to assure us equality in the pursuit of happiness. We have come to a clear realization of the fact that true individual freedom cannot exist without economic security and independence. "Necessitous men are not free men." People who are hungry and out of a job are the stuff of which dictatorships are made...

I ask the Congress to explore the means for implementing this economic bill of rights...

> - *The right to a useful and remunerative job in the industries or shops or farms or mines of the Nation*
> - *The right to earn enough to provide adequate food and clothing and recreation*
> - *The right of every farmer to raise and sell his products at a return which will give him and his family a decent living*
> - *The right of every businessman, large and small, to trade in an atmosphere of freedom from unfair competition and domination by monopolies at home or abroad*
> - *The right of every family to a decent home*
> - *The right to adequate medical care and the opportunity to achieve and enjoy good health*
> - *The right to adequate protection from the economic fears of old age, sickness, accident, and unemployment*
> - *The right to a good education*

These rights were embraced by the United Nations, India, Europe, and post-apartheid South Africa, for all citizens. The U.S. Congress tossed some scraps of these rights to some citizens in the G.I. Bill of 1944. Much of American history afterwards has been a war over the survival and extension of those rights.

> *Now we are asking you to get yourselves killed, but we promise you that when you have done this, you will keep yours jobs until the end of your lives.*
>
> *Social pacts of a kind that promised—to those who were asked to go to war and get themselves killed—a certain type of economic and social organization which assured security (of employment, with regard to illness and other kinds of risk, and at the level of retirement) ...*
>
> *The demand for war on the part of governments is accompanied ... by this offer of a social pact and security.*
> —Michel Foucault, *THE BIRTH OF BIOPOLITICS*

TRUMAN

The trend towards concentration of power in the executive branch was somewhat slowed when FDR died in 1945 and was replaced by Harry Truman. In 1951, Republicans helped pass the TWENTY-SECOND AMENDMENT to the Constitution, in hopes of controlling any FDRs of the future. Roosevelt had been elected to four terms, and this Amendment restricted any future President to only two.

HARRY TRUMAN

In 1952, the Supreme Court told Truman that, Korean War or no, he had to go to Congress before he could begin seizing steel mills to stop a labor dispute *(Youngstown Sheet and Tube Co. v. Sawyer* [1952]).

Nevertheless, executive power continued to grow. On his own initiative, Truman dropped atomic bombs on Japan, sent troops to Korea, and desegregated the armed forces. During this tenure, executive agencies like the Council of Economic Advisors, the National Security Council, and the Bureau of Budget (now the OMB) were created. In addition, Truman established a loyalty board which evaluated over 4.25 million federal employees during 1947-1953.

RED SCARES

One reason Americans accepted this employment of power passed under the phrase "national emergency." World War II had ended in 1945. But with Hitler gone, Stalin soon took his place as the international boogeyman. It was during this period that Americans began to accept the notion that Members of Congress could not engage in controversies over foreign policy during periods of undeclared war without being called traitors. "Bipartisanship" was the label used to describe this phenomenon. Both parties were expected to line up behind the President, no matter what he wanted to do with the country in foreign affairs.

In addition to being cited as justification for growing presidential power, these magic words were also used to justify many congressional actions that would delight the most dedicated totalitarian. In 1950, the INTERNAL SECURITY ACT established a Subversive Activities Control Board, along with six concentration camps for political undesirables in case of an "internal security emergency". In 1954, the Communist Party was outlawed. Politicians used congressional investigating power, congressional immunity, FBI informers, local red squads, and cheap theater, to smear and intimidate political opponents, government workers, union officials, teachers and artists, driving many to unemployment, social ostracism, divorce, deportation, heart attacks and suicide.

The issue between Republicans and Democrats is clearly drawn: it has been deliberately drawn by those that have been in charge of twenty years of treason.
—Senator Joseph R. McCarthy, 1952 G.O.P. Convention

117

The Supreme Court generally did little to interpose the Bill of Rights between the witch hunters and their victims: *American Communication Association v. Douds* (1950), *Dennis v. U.S.* (1951), *Bailey v. Richardson* (1951), *contrast Joint Anti-Fascist Committee v. McGrath* (1951).

It was not until the second half of the decade that this trend changed. *Quinn v. U.S. (1955), Peters v. Hobby* (1956), *Cole v. Young* (1956), *Yates v. U.S.* (1957), *Watkins v. U.S.* (1957).

There were at least two reasons underlying the Court's eventual shift. First, the nation's appetite for Joe McCarthy proved limited, and after the Senate's censure of him (Dec. 2, 1954), the Supreme Court felt safe to oppose red-baiting (a tactic of claiming, often without any evidence, that a political opponent was communist or socialist, in order to damage his or her career). The second big reason was that Earl Warren had been appointed Chief Justice.

EARL WARREN

The good news about Earl Warren was that he promulgated a vision of the Constitution which ensured that it would be interpreted as a guarantor of democracy and human rights. The bad news was that he was so effective many people began to look to the Court (instead of themselves) as the source of their political good fortunes. They started giving their problems to lawyers, asking them to solve things in courtrooms, instead of taking to the streets. In any case, the impact of the Warren Court on America's constitutional order is impossible to dispute.

Warren was a Republican from California, appointed to the Chief Justice position by Dwight Eisenhower. In part, the appointment was a reward for Warren's help in securing Ike the presidential nomination in 1952. In part, it was an attempt to kick Warren upstairs, and get him out of California, so that Vice President Nixon's minions could enjoy more power in that state's G.O.P.

Whatever Eisenhower might have expected of Warren, he was unpleasantly surprised. When asked if he had made any mistakes during his administration, Eisenhower replied, "Yes, two, and they are both sitting on the Supreme Court." (The other "mistake" was William Brennan).

One of the first things Warren did when he assumed his seat was engineer possibly the most significant decision of his 16 years on the Court, viz., *Brown v. Board of Education.*

COME BACK YOU!

EARL WARREN

Liberal Territory

DWIGHT EISENHOWER

BROWN V. BOARD OF EDUCATION

In *Brown,* black schoolchildren challenged the "separate but equal" educational facilities that the state of Kansas was supposedly giving them pursuant to segregation sanctioned by *Plessy v. Ferguson. Brown* was already before the Supreme Court when Warren assumed his role as Chief Justice. The justices could not agree whether to overrule *Plessy* outright, or simply to enforce the "equal" part of the "separate but equal" doctrine. Four justices preferred the latter course, in part because they had been doing that for years, and in part because they feared the political uproar that was bound to follow if they overruled *Plessy.*

According to Justice William O. Douglas, Warren's skillful organizing transformed a potentially divisive 5-4 vote into a 9-0 unanimous vote:

> *The fact that a worldly and wise man like Warren would stake his reputation on this issue not only impressed Frankfurter but seemed to have a like influence on Reed and Clark. Clark followed shortly, Reed finally came around somewhat doubtfully, and only Jackson was left.*

ROBERT JACKSON

EARL WARREN

Warren visited Jackson, who was recuperating from a heart attack in the hospital.

Jackson had said to count him in, which made the opinion unanimous. We could present a solid front to the country, and it was a brilliant diplomatic process which Warren had engineered.

Brown held that not only was Kansas being unequal; the separation of the races was itself inherently unequal:

We conclude that in the field of public education, the doctrine of "separate but equal" has no place. Separate educational facilities are inherently unequal.

The short term significance of the *Brown* decision lay in its explicit repudiation of *Plessy* and its 50-plus years of state-sponsored racism. The long-term significance of *Brown* lay in the constitutional upheavals which it unleashed.

REACTIONS

The political turmoil anticipated by the more conservative justices was not long in coming. Many southern states passed resolutions and laws defying the Supreme Court. In 1957, President Eisenhower had to send federal troops into Little Rock, Arkansas, to keep order when nine African American students were both barred by the state's National Guard from entering a segregated school and threatened by an angry mob. In the litigation following the Little Rock crisis, the Supreme Court cited *Marbury v. Madison* to the effect that "this decision declared the basic principle that the federal judiciary is supreme in the exposition of the law of the Constitution." More dubiously, it asserted that "this principle has ever since been respected by this Court and the Country as a permanent and indispensable feature of our constitutional system."

LITTLE ROCK 1957

Whatever words the Supreme Court might write in its decisions, by the early 1960s, it had achieved only limited success in eliminating institutionalized racism in the South. School desegregation had slowed, from some 750 systems desegregated during the first four years after *Brown*, to 49 for the following three.

The Supreme Court and the Interstate Commerce Commission both declared that buses travelling across state lines should be integrated. Freedom Riders testing these propositions in 1961 were brutally beaten:

> *In South Carolina... there were several young white hoodlums... and they blocked the door and said "Nigger, you can't come in here."*
>
> *He said, "I have every right to enter this waiting room according to the Supreme Court of the United States in the Boynton case."*
>
> *They said, "Shit on that."*
>
> *He tried to walk past, and they clubbed him, beat him, and knocked him down.*
>
> *–James Farmer, Civil Rights Activist*

Even in Montgomery, Alabama, site of the successful boycotts of 1955-1956, segregated customs were returning to the buses.

BLACK MOBILIZATION

The broader effects of the *Brown* decision finally came when civil rights supporters managed to mobilize (i) blacks; (ii) whites; and (iii) the executive branch of the federal government.

The first happened when groups like the STUDENT NON-VIOLENT COORDINATING COMMITTEE abandoned the litigating strategies of the NATIONAL ASSOCIATION FOR THE ADVANCEMENT OF COLORED PEOPLE and engaged in civil disobedience and community organizing.

The second happened when civil rights organizers realized that racists shooting at whites would disgust the rest of the country more thoroughly than racists shooting at blacks:

They were not gonna respond to a thousand blacks working in that area [Mississippi]. They would respond to a thousand young white college students, and white college females who were down there... the death of a white college student would bring more attention to what was going on than for a black college student getting it. That's cold, but that was also in another sense speaking the language of this country. —Dave Dennis, Civil Rights Activist

The third happened when President John F. Kennedy realized two things:

— FIRST, his electoral victory depended upon blacks in the north. He carried Illinois by only 9,000 votes, where 250,000 blacks had voted for him. Michigan was carried by 67,000 votes, where another 250,000 blacks were estimated to have voted for JFK. Some 40,000 blacks were the key to his 10,000-vote margin in South Carolina.

— SECOND, America's position abroad depended upon people's perception of how the USA treated its black population.

Three weeks after Oxford [where Kennedy sent troops to protect James Meredith, a black student attempting to attend college in Mississippi], Sekou Toure and Ben Bella [African leaders] were prepared to deny refueling facilities to Soviet planes bound for Cuba during the missile crisis. —Arthur Schlesinger, Presidential Aide

With these mobilizations, the Constitution was amended in 1964 with AMENDMENT TWENTY-FOUR, which eliminated the poll tax which anti-Populist Bourbons had used to discourage poor blacks (and whites) from voting. In 1961 The District of Columbia had been given electoral votes by the TWENTY-THIRD AMENDMENT).

24th Amendment

Additionally, Congress passed a number of Civil Rights measures, particularly the CIVIL RIGHTS ACT OF 1964, which prohibited segregation in public accommodations. The 1965 VOTING RIGHTS ACT was aimed at other Bourbon measures used to limit black voting, including registration requirements and literacy tests.

CHILDREN...

While minorities demonstrated and rioted because they were tired of apartheid in the South and ghettoes in the North, students did the same because they were tired of being drafted to kill and die in Vietnam.

Vietnam, unfortunately, was one more example of many wars in which the USA used troops without a formal, constitutional declaration of war. As early as 1854, President Franklin Pierce sent troops to Nicaragua without congressional authorization. Wilson sent troops to Mexico, Eisenhower did it in Lebanon, and Johnson did it in the Dominican Republic. Kennedy began the process, for both Johnson and Nixon, in Vietnam.

One problem with Vietnam was that it took too much time, money and blood. In 1963, the USA had 16,000 "advisers" in Vietnam; by 1969 they had turned into 542,000 soldiers. By 1973, 51,000 of them had been killed, and another 270,000 wounded. The Vietnam price tag further involved $150 billion, 570,000 draft offenders and 563,000 less-than-honorable discharges from the military. On the Vietnamese side, casualties approached levels of genocide and ecocide. Young Americans got sick of being drafted into a dubious cause that made them into cannon-fodder (and sometimes war criminals).They found it particularly obnoxious that if you were between 18 and 21, you could be drafted to war, but not vote. The country tried to resolve this conundrum in 1971 with the TWENTY-SIXTH AMENDMENT, which reduced the voting age to 18 years.

...AND WOMEN

EQUAL RIGHTS AMENDMENT

On the home front, women grew tired of being caged in their kitchens to live as barefoot baby-machines. Discrimination against persons on the basis of sex had been outlawed in the Civil Rights Act of 1964; but at the time not many took it seriously because a southern congressperson had pushed it to "prove" the "nonsense" of outlawing discrimination on the basis of race. As the 1960s proceeded, women started their own protests. In 1972, Congress passed Title IX, which outlawed sex discrimination in education (including sports). In 1973, the Supreme Court rendered *Roe v. Wade*, which held that women had some rights when it came to using their bodies to make babies. Like discrimination based on race, discrimination based on sex had become serious business.

In 1923, an equal rights amendment to the U.S. Constitution was proposed. In 1972 Congress submitted it to the states for ratification. At this time of this writing, the ERA still stands three states short of becoming a constitutional amendment.

MORE JUDICIAL PROGRESS

Against this background of democratic upheaval, the Warren Court instituted a number of other reforms in America's constitutional order.

— Individuals held to have a right to form groups for political purposes, *NAACP v. Alabama* (1957).

— Police forced to gather evidence properly, prohibited from using materials obtained during unreasonable searches and seizures *Mapp v. Ohio* (1961).

— Schools stopped from forcing children to pray. *Engele v. Vitale* (1962)..

> *After his retirement, Chief Justice Earl Warren was asked what he regarded to be the decision during his tenure that would have the greatest consequence for all Americans. His choice was Baker v. Carr, because he believed that if each of us has an equal vote, we are equally armed with the indispensible means to make our views felt.*
> —*Justice William Brennan*

— States forced to apportion their legislative districts on a "one man one vote" basis *Baker v. Carr* (1962), *Reynolds v. Sims* (1964).

FOLLOWING "ONE MAN ONE VOTE" A DISTRICT OF FOR EXAMPLE 100 PEOPLE SHOULD NOT CARRY THE SAME WEIGHT AS ONE WITH 1000.

- States required to provide criminal defendants with counsel if they were unable to pay for one, *Gideon v. Wainwright* (1963).
- Right to privacy recognized (also allowing a couple to receive birth control information without governmental interference), *Griswold v. Connecticut* (1965).
- Police told to read suspects their rights *Miranda v. Arizona* (1966).

The net result was a system more solicitous of the rights of individuals and minorities, and more open to democratic transformation.

REACTION REDUX

TIDES OF HISTORY

The reader who has been paying attention can probably guess what happened after the 1960s. American history has a pattern of push and pull between democracy and reaction. After the unruly Revolution came the orderly Constitution; after Jefferson, the South tried to expand its slave empire. After the Civil War and Reconstruction, the nation entered the Gilded Age. World War I helped end the Progressive Era. FDR's New Deal is something the Republicans have been fighting since it arose. With Reagan and the Bushes, they achieved some victories for the wealthy.

Presidents throughout American history have pointed out this fundamental conflict which occurs regularly within the Republic:

> One of the divisions consists of those, who... are more partial to the opulent... The other division consists of those who [hate] hereditary power as an insult to the reason and an outrage to the rights of man. —James Madison, 1792

...two opposing principles that have been in active operation in this country from the closing scenes of the revolutionary war[sic] to the present day—the one seeking to absorb, as far as practicable, all power from its legitimate sources, and to condense it in a single head. The other, an antagonist principle, laboring as assiduously to resist the encroachments and limit the extent of executive authority... The former is essentially the monarchical, the latter the democratical spirit, of society. —Martin Van Buren, 1828

Martin Van Buren

The [Democrats] of today hold the liberty of one man to be absolutely nothing, when in conflict with another man's right of property. Republicans, on the contrary, are for both the man and the dollar; but in cases of conflict, the man before the dollar. —Abraham Lincoln, 1859

...if history were to repeat itself and we were to return to the so-called "normalcy" of the 1920s—then it is certain that even though we shall have conquered our enemies on the battlefields abroad, we shall have yielded to the spirit of Fascism here at home. —Franklin D. Roosevelt, 1944

In the councils of government, we must guard against the acquisition of unwarranted influence, whether sought or unsought, by the military-industrial complex... We must never let the weight of this combination endanger our liberties or democratic processes. —Dwight Eisenhower, 1961

131

REACTION RE-ORGANIZES

In August 1971, through the U.S. Chamber of Commerce, he circulated a "confidential" memo concerning attacks on the "free enterprise" system and how to save it:

Two months later, Nixon nominated Lewis Powell to the U.S. Supreme Court, and three months after that, Congress confirmed his appointment. More significantly, wealthy individuals and corporations began to finance the creation of organizations to mobilize the Right:

RICHARD NIXON

LEWIS POWELL

> *Survival of what we call the free enterprise system lies in organization, in careful long-range planning and implementation, in consistency of action over an indefinite period of years, in the scale of financing available only through joint effort, and in the political power available only through united action and national organizations.* —Lewis Powell

1972— Ford Foundation grant revives American Enterprise Institute
1972— Corporate executives establish Business Roundtable
1973— Heritage Foundation founded, subsidized by Coors and Mellon heir Scaife
1974— Committee for the Survival of a Free Congress (more Coors money)
1974— Conservative Caucus founded
1977— Cato Institute founded with money from Charles Koch, wealthy Kansas businessman
1978— National Conservative Political Action Committee founded
1979— Moral Majority founded
1982— Federalist Society founded

The above helped revive the military industrial complex as well as the money, privilege, monarchy and opulence that was the catalyst for, and the reoccurring point of contention since the adoption of, the Constitution.

THE NIXON WAVE

For his part, Richard Nixon made a run at equaling Shakespeare's "Richard III" by bringing power in the executive branch to new levels of large quantity and lousy quality. He increased the White House staff from 1700 to 2500. He impounded monies appropriated by Congress, preventing them from spending money on programs he did not like. Some presidents had done this sparingly in the past; the enabling legislation gave some discretion. Contrary to laws enacted by Congress, Nixon announced he would no longer enforce Title VI of the 1964 Civil Rights Act, which directed that government funds could not go to institutions practicing discrimination; and, he attempted to dismantle the Office of Economic Opportunity.

He also expanded the Vietnam War into Cambodia (1970), and helped overthrow the democratically elected government of Chile (1973).

4th AMENDMENT? OH YOU MEAN MY NEW CARPET.

4th Amendment

Nixon took his claims of executive power so seriously he had his lawyers tell the courts he could ignore the Fourth Amendment's search and seizure clauses in the interests of "national security." He established a "Plumbers" unit to spy on Americans he did not like, and on June 17, 1972, these heroes were caught with wire-tapping equipment in the Democratic Party Headquarters in the Watergate Hotel. On June 19, 1972, the Supreme Court overruled Nixon's rejection of the Fourth Amendment.

Subsequent court hearings indicated that the White House had been involved in the Watergate break-in. The Senate created a Selected Committee, and later an Office of Special Prosecutor (to be appointed by Nixon), to investigate. Various incidents of White House corruption and abuse of power in violation of constitutionally-guaranteed rights came to light. In summer 1973 it was learned that Nixon had been making tapes of White House conversations since 1971, and that 18 minutes from the June 20, 1972, tapes had been suspiciously erased. The first Special Prosecutor (Archibald Cox) asked for Nixon's tapes, to see how deeply Nixon had involved himself in obstruction of justice. Nixon had to fire two attorneys-general (Elliot Richardson and William Ruckelshaus) before he found a man sufficiently debased (Robert Bork) to fire Cox (October 1973). After this "Saturday Night Massacre", the House began impeachment proceedings, and, in November, Nixon made his famous announcement that he was "not a crook." In March 1974, the new Special Prosecutor reiterated the demand for the tapes, and on July 24, 1974, the U.S. Supreme Court told Nixon his "executive privilege" claims were bogus. Nixon released the tapes. They showed clearly that, on June 23, 1972, he had, in fact, authorized the CIA to obstruct the Watergate investigation—and justice.

Rather than face impeachment and removal from office, Nixon became the first President in American history to resign.

IM READY FOR MY CLOSE UP.

THE REAGAN (COUNTER) REVOLUTION

The next big pushes for militarism, monarchy and money occurred under Ronald Reagan and George Bush. Less grotesque than Nixon, they nevertheless maintained and expanded his legacy.

When Reagan took office (1981), he continued the drive for executive power, despite his small-government rhetoric. He used the Justice Department in actions against local affirmative action programs, and in *Bob Jones v. U.S.* (1983).

In 1983, Reagan invaded Grenada two days after being embarrassed by a bombing of U.S. troops in Lebanon. In 1985, he declared an emergency over share-the-wealth types (called Sandinistas) who had taken over the government in Nicaragua.

On the judicial front, Reagan attempted to appoint people that were both ideological and young. On the ideological front, his Attorney General, Ed Meese, began hollering that federal judges should follow the "original intent" of the Founding Framers when they framed the Constitution. This supposed "doctrine of judicial construction" was, of course, nothing but ideology dressed in fancy words. As a matter

136

of common sense, a judge invents as much as when he images what a bunch of dead men thought in 1789 as what he or she thinks is appropriate 200 years later. As a matter of history, "original intent" contravened the Framers' notion that the Constitution should change and grow with human experience.

"LAWS AND INSTITUTIONS MUST GO HAND IN HAND WITH THE PROGRESS OF THE HUMAN MIND."

COULD YOU COPY JOHN ADAMS AND MYSELF ON THAT EMAIL?

In the draught of a fundamental constitution, it is necessary to insert essential principles only, lest the operations of government should be clogged by rendering those provisions permanent and unalterable, which ought to be accommodated to times and events...
—*Edmund Randolph, one of five charged with drafting the Constitution*

[The Constitution is] intended to endure for ages to come, and, consequently, to be adapted to the various CRISES of human affairs.
—*John Marshall, first influential Chief Justice of Supreme Court*

...laws and institutions must go hand in hand with the progress of the human mind. As that becomes more developed, more enlightened, as new discoveries are made, new truths disclosed, and manners and opinions change with the change of circumstances, institutions must advance also, and keep pace with the times.
—*Thomas Jefferson, (look at your nickel, or check your two-dollar bill)*

Reagan's version of Watergate was "Irangate," which grew out of Reagan's brave efforts to send weaponry to Iran's Ayatolla Khomeni in exchange for American hostages. Somewhere along the line, some of the profits from these transactions were skimmed, and sent to Reagan's "contras" in Central America, in violation of various congressional mandates. Reports began to surface that the contras were running drugs, and that money from their supporters was being used to defeat candidates opposed to Reagan's aggressions in Nicaragua. The constitutional questions, of course, involved the extent to which the American people and their so-called representatives would call upon the President to obey the laws of the land, like any other citizen—laws which he had sworn to uphold, unlike many other citizens. But Reagan said he was sorry (March 1987) and Congress said it couldn't tell what really happened because Reagan's flunkies had shredded too many documents (November, 1987).

Perhaps it is fitting that when Nixon's Lewis Powell retired from the Supreme Court in 1987, Reagan tried to replace him with Robert Bork, hero of Nixon's Saturday Night Massacre. The Senate rejected Bork.

H.W. BUSH AND SADDAM'S
THE ODD COUPLE

In 1988, George Bush was elected President. In four years, he managed to invade Panama and depose dictator Noriega (1989). After encouraging Saddam Hussein to take Kuwait (1990), Bush changed his mind and invaded Iraq (1991); but balked at deposing Saddam. In 1992, Bush pardoned Reagan officials associated with Irangate, including Reagan's Secretary of Defense (Weinberger).

138

THE 20th CENTURY ENDS

GINGRICH   CLINTON

The American people voted for a change of pace with the election of Bill Clinton in 1992, but the moneyed and privileged crowd never stopped trying. In 1994, led by Newt Gingrich, Republicans took Congress; and in 1995 they tried to force Clinton to sign a rightwing budget by withholding funds and suspending governmental operations. Clinton won that showdown, but unfortunately, his well-publicized affair with Monica Lewinsky hampered his efforts through the rest of his presidency. In 1998, Republicans in the House then tried to impeach Clinton for lying about his affair, even though the year exposed many of them as experts in adultery themselves, including House Speaker Robert Livingston, House leader Henry Hyde, and vocal critics like Dan Burton and Helen Chenoweth. Newt Gingrich later confessed to having an affair during the impeachment carnival, "partially driven by how passionately I felt about this country." (yes, his words).

In the year 2000, the money and privilege crowd made its ultimate grab for power, when 5 conservatives on the U.S. Supreme Court gave the Presidency to George W. Bush, son of George Bush. Even though the State of Florida was still figuring out how to count its vote, the conservative majority jettisoned its solicitude over states' rights and awarded Florida's votes to Bush, giving him enough to put him into the White House.

THE COUNTRY IS YOURS NOW KID.

BUSH JR.

139

The individual citizen has no federal constitutional right to vote for electors for the President of the United States unless and until the state legislature chooses a statewide election as the means to implement its power to appoint members of the Electoral College... Our consideration is limited to the present circumstances, for the problem of equal protection in election processes generally presents many complexities.... None are more conscious of the vital limits on judicial authority than are the members of this Court, and none stand more in admiration of the Constitution's design to leave the selection of the President to the people, through their legislatures, and to the political sphere. When contending parties invoke the process of the courts, however, it becomes our unsought responsibility to resolve the federal and constitutional issues the judicial system has been forced to confront.
—Bush v. Gore, Per curium (Latin for "by the court," defining a decision of an appeals court as a whole in which no judge is identified as the specific author— which makes sense for a decision no self-respecting judge would want to sign)

What must underlie petitioners' entire federal assault on the Florida election procedures is an unstated lack of confidence in the impartiality and capacity of the state judges who would make the critical decisions if the vote count were to proceed. Otherwise, their position is wholly without merit. The endorsement of that position by the majority of this Court can only lend credence to the most cynical appraisal of the work of judges throughout the land. It is confidence in the men and women who administer the judicial system that is the true backbone of the rule of law. Time will one day heal the wound to that confidence that will be inflicted by today's decision. One thing, however, is certain. Although we may never know with complete certainty the identity of the winner of this year's Presidential election, the identity of the loser is perfectly clear. It is the Nation's confidence in the judge as an impartial guardian of the rule of law.
—Bush v. Gore, Justice John Paul Stevens, dissenting, and, per usual and per self-respect signing his name to it

THE 21st CENTURY BEGINS

On September 11, 2001, Muslim fanatics flew two airplanes into the World Trade Center buildings in Manhattan. G.W. Bush followed the footsteps of Woodrow Wilson. The American population was disciplined through the Patriot Act, which expanded government authority to wiretap, detain and deport immigrants, investigate libraries, and search phone, e-mail, medical, and financial records. The American oil interests were given the invasion of Afghanistan and occupation of Iraq.

THE PATRIOT ACT
WATCHES US ALWAYS

> *"Ever since the continents started interacting politically, some 500 years ago, Eurasia has been the center of world power."*
> —*Zbigniew Brzezinski, National Security Advisor to Democratic President Jimmy Carter, 1997*

G.W. Bush continued his father's practice of denigrating affirmative action through affirmative mockery. Just as George I nominated Clarence Thomas (an under-qualified African American candidate) to the Supreme Court, George II nominated an under-qualified woman candidate, Harriet Myers (even conservatives protested). To head the Justice Department, G.W. Bush appointed Latino

Alberto Gonzales, who was eventually forced to resign because he pushed Justice Department appointees to work according to a standard of political correctness (as opposed to legal integrity). For example, nine U.S. Attorneys were fired in December 2006 because they had been "lax" in prosecuting supposedly fraudulent voting efforts by potential Democratic activists.

By the time G.W. Bush left office in 2009, it was not clear what was left of the U.S. Constitution; or the City of New Orleans (wrecked by Katrina); or the American Empire (subservient to Chinese loans); or Anglo-Saxon anarcho-capitalism (reliant on U.S. taxpayer bailouts). Yet the privileged who put down their money during the 1970s did have a few things to show for their organizational investments:

- "In 2007, CEOs at major U.S. corporations were being paid 344 times the pay of the average worker," twice as much as their European counterparts, 9 times as much as their Japanese counterparts, and much better than 1980, when they made only 42 times what the average American worker made. (Sandel)

- Under G.W. Bush, tax rates on the wealthiest Americans were limited to 35%, down from 50% under Reagan, 70% under Nixon, and 91% under Eisenhower.

- In 1981 the top 1% owned 25% of the wealth; and by 2009 it had moved to 38%.

When liberty is skewed into the hands of a very small number of the population, then our ability to "self-govern" becomes a complete and utter illusion.
—Ron Paul, fringe Republican, 2009

What Americans were going to do with their constitutional order after the election of Barack Obama in 2008 remained to be seen. The money and privilege crowd did not go to sleep. Like the Federalists who opposed Jefferson, they enjoyed their judicial "stronghold" as a "battery." In *Timmons v. Twin Cities Area New Party,* (1997) the Supreme Court took sides with the southern Bourbons from the 1890s, and Court denied that citizens had any right to "fusion" voting, (Recall that this technical, important, and inconvenient rule encourages formation of third and fourth parties—and thus more voter viewpoints, interest and participation. In *Crawford v. Marion County Election Board (2008),* the Supreme Court allowed states impose photo ID restrictions on voters, adversely impacting low income and minority voters. In *Citizens United v. FEC (2010)*, the Supreme Court held that corporations had First Amendment rights to fund independent political broadcasts in candidate elections. (The fact that the election of 2008 had the highest voter participation since the 1960s had nothing to do with these decisions, of course). The benefits of these decisions began to show in 2010 when Republicans re-took the House of Representatives.

In their fine documentary THE CORPORATION, Mark Achbar, Jennifer Abbott and Joel Bakan take modern law at its word and ask, "If the corporation were a person, what sort of person would it be?" Using the American Psychiatric Association's Diagnostic and Statistical Manual of Mental Disorders (DSM-IV) to match behavior against a list of symptoms, they find that corporations exhibit many of the characteristics that define psychopaths. The American Psychiatric Association classifies psychopaths and sociopaths under the general diagnosis of "antisocial personality disorder," and to be diagnosed with the disorder, the patient needs to meet three out of these seven criteria:

1. Failure to conform to social norms with respect to lawful behaviors as indicated by repeatedly performing acts that are grounds for arrest

2. Deceitfulness, as indicated by repeated lying, use of aliases, or conning others for personal profit or pleasure

3. Impulsivity or failure to plan ahead

4. Irritability and aggressiveness, as indicated by repeated physical fights or assaults

5 Reckless disregard for safety of self or others

6. Consistent irresponsibility, as indicated by repeated failure to sustain consistent work behavior or honor financial obligations

7. Lack of remorse, as indicated by being indifferent to or rationalizing having hurt, mistreated, or stolen from another

EVALUATION

So how has the Constitution done? The Framers themselves have set the standards. Criteria for evaluating their product were articulated in the Preamble. The success of the Constitution rises or falls according to these benchmarks. We can see what the Framers intended, what happened over time, how things stand today, and grade accordingly.

We the People of the United States,

The good news is that when the Framers wrote "we the people" they meant mainly white males who owned property. Now, people understand "we the people" to mean every adult citizen, regardless of sex, race, wealth or creed.

The less good news is how "we the people" has been and is being defined as a matter of general law, and as a matter of election law. In 1886, the Supreme Court held that corporations were "persons" and since then has used this concept to stop real people from regulating them. In 2010 this concept was expanded to ensure that corporations could, as persons of the United States, use their financial power to influence election campaigns.

While the status of corporations as part of "we the people" grows more secure, the status of real human persons has varied. We have seen that around 1900, Bourbons used poll taxes and literacy tests to limit voting by poor blacks and whites. Around 2000, the Supreme Court was sanctioning similar tricks with restrictions on forming third parties and voting at the polls—for everybody.

So at this point "we the people" is bigger than what it was in 1787, but it's a pretty complicated and convoluted "people".

in Order to form a more perfect Union,

For the Framers (as reported by the French Ambassador), a "more perfect union" meant "a Federal Government [with] more energy and vigor," resulting in "a regular collecting of taxes, a severe administration of justice, extraordinary rights on imports, rigorous actions against debtors, and lastly a marked preponderance of rich men and property owners."

146

In general the Framers got what they wanted, but holding Americans together under this centralized authority has not always been easy. New England wanted to secede in 1814-1815. South Carolina wanted to nullify in 1832-1833. The South did secede in 1860-1861. Scam elections were needed in 1876 and 2000. Today people wonder how Massachusetts and Mississippi can fly under the same flag. Maybe they're right. Europe is working to provide an alternative model of federalism.

establish Justice,

Justice involves a fair allocation of reward and punishment. Certainly the Framers believed it would be unfair if THEIR goods would be re-allocated according to "a leveling spirit." To a degree they have succeeded, what with the invention of the corporation as an infinite vehicle for wealth accumulation. To a degree they have failed, what with things like the income tax (1913), social security (1935), and Medicare (1965). However, the tax cut and privatization crowd continues to work at eliminating all three.

Any remarks on justice in the United States cannot ignore the fact that in 1787 the Constitution thought it was just fine to use slavery to steal work product from African Americans. A civil war decided that this form of exchange was invalid, to the tune of $800 million. After the civil war, whites used sharecropping, lynching, and racism to steal work product from African Americans.

With approximately 2.3 million people in prison or jail, the United States incarcerates more people than any other country in the world—by far...
Blacks are incarcerated at a rate eight times higher than that of whites ... —David Cole

The Shays rebellion inspired five states in Annapolis (1786) to grow to twelve states in Philadelphia the following year. The Framers marked it as a success that guns created tranquility with the suppression of a similar Whiskey Rebellion after the institution of their Constitution. Guns have been creating tranquility in the United States ever since. U.S. labor history has been characterized as the "bloodiest and most violent" of any industrial nation in the world. The moderate historian Richard Hofstadter (who noted the preceding) has also observed that our civil strife "rather resembles some Latin American Republics or the volatile new states of Asia and Africa." He also notes the biased ways it has been used to benefit the establishment, which explains why "in turn it has been so easily and indulgently forgotten."

provide for the common defense,

The United States has never lost a war where it was defending its own territories. But we are talking defense, here, and one has to question how the U.S. has come to define the term. "National security" now seems to include addiction to foreign oil and Asian loans. Beyond that, concepts of defense have been expanded to include the right to send troops into black ghettoes, college campuses, perimeters around GOP convention sites, Cuba, the Philippines, Mexico, Korea, Vietnam, the Dominican Republic, Lebanon, Grenada, Iraq and Afghanistan; sponsor the overthrow of governments in Hawaii, Chile, Cuba, Guatemala and Angola; drop mines in the waters of Nicaragua; drop bombs on Libya; go to war over gasoline in the Persian Gulf; go to "war on drugs" everywhere; sell guns anywhere; train local militaries in "internal defense" (or, "state terrorism") in over 150 nations; maintain more than 725 military bases around the world; spend more money on "defense" than the next 15 nations combined; spend more money than can even be accounted for; and pile enough nuclear weapons to exterminate civilization many times over (although once would presumably suffice). Such an expansive concept of defense probably does more to subvert "the common defense" than to enhance it. How much the Framers wanted U.S. defense to be provided by private contractors raises yet another question.

We cannot say the founders did not warn us:

1787: No money shall be drawn from the Treasury, but in Consequence of Appropriations made by Law; and a regular Statement and Account of the Receipts and Expenditures of all public Money shall be published from time to time. —Art. 1, Sec. 9, clause 7, U.S. Const

1788: Not the less true is it, that the liberties of Rome proved the final victim to her military triumphs; and that the liberties of Europe, as far as they ever existed, have, with few exceptions, been the price of her military establishments. A standing force, therefore, is a dangerous, at the same time that it may be a necessary, provision. On the smallest scale it has its inconveniences. On an extensive scale its consequences may be fatal. —Federalist No. 41

1793: In no part of the Constitution is more wisdom to be found than in the clause which confides the questions of war or peace to the legislature, not the executive department... War is in fact the true nurse of executive aggrandizement... Hence it has grown into an axiom that the executive is the department of power most distinguished by its propensity to war: hence it is the practice of all states, in proportion as they are free, to disarm this propensity of its influence. —James Madison

1796: Overgrown military establishments are under any form of government inauspicious to liberty, and are to be regarded as particularly hostile to Republican liberty.
—George Washington

promote the general Welfare,

The United States is wealthy. It has produced the most substantial Gross National Product in the history of the world. So the welfare is there, but how generally has it been spread around is another matter entirely.

Economist Jeff Madrick has noted that while the USA leads OECD (Organization for Economic Co-operation and Development) nations in income and wealth, it also leads them in inequality, poverty, crime, hours worked, and infant mortality.

Anthropologist Frans de Wall (who knows monkeys) has observed:

> *The United States used to have the world's healthiest and tallest citizens, but now ranks at the bottom among industrialized nations in terms of longevity and height and at the top in terms of teenage pregnancy and infant mortality. Whereas most nations have been adding nearly one inch per decade to their average height, the United States has not done so since the 1970s. The result is that Northern Europeans now tower on average three inches over Americans. This isn't explained by recent United States immigrants, which constitute too tiny a fraction of the population to affect these statistics. In terms of life expectancy, too, the United States is not keeping up with the rest of the world. On this critical health index, Americans don't even rank among the top twenty-five nations anymore.*

So regardless of whatever trends the Framers may have successfully promoted in 1789, by 2000 the *general* welfare of American bodies seems to have dissipated.

Another matter of general welfare involves the environment that American bodies inhabit. The Framers' constitutional order has been manipulated to allow fictional beings which do not have to face death (i.e., corporations) to frame the debate, define the terms, and restrict the meaning of "general welfare" when it comes to planet earth. One dissenting Supreme Court Justice did try to address the issue in 1972:

151

> *The corporation sole — a creature of ecclesiastical law — is an acceptable adversary and large fortunes ride on its cases.... So it should be as respects valleys, alpine meadows, rivers, lakes, estuaries, beaches, ridges, groves of trees, swampland, or even air that feels the destructive pressures of modern technology and modern life.*
> —William O. Douglas, SIERRA V. MORTON dissenting, 1972

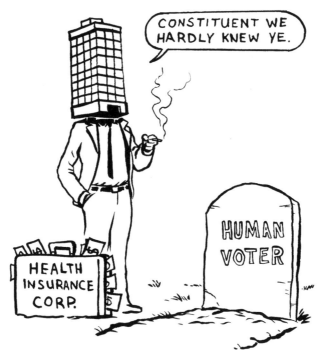

A final matter of general welfare involves the creation of culture and inventions for the public good. In Art. I, Sec. 8, Clause 8, the Constitution's Copyright and Patent Clause empowers Congress "to promote the Progress of Science and useful Arts, by securing for limited Times to Authors and Inventors the exclusive Right to their respective Writings and Discoveries." Perhaps the reader should wait some years before giving a grade in this area: she will want to see where the system has drawn property lines for things like health drugs, life forms (seeds), cultural forms (Mickey Mouse), human genes, sunshine, air, water, etc., etc.

Secure the Blessings of Liberty to ourselves and our Posterity

The Framers knew that liberty was an issue for the American people, and so they quickly added the Bill of Rights to the Constitution to raise the odds that it would be accepted. Yet rights on paper are one thing, rights in practice are another.

The history of civil liberties across the world seems to indicate that the less threats a nation experiences, the better is its record on civil liberties. Thus England, an island protected by water, has done relatively well. Surrounded by two big oceans and two weak nations, the United States too has done rather well. Generally, it rates highly on Amnesty International's list (except for capital punishment), and most American are rightly proud of the freedoms they enjoy from day to day.

Yet the American Bill of Rights does NOT contain certain provisions set out in the UN Declaration of Rights (e.g., the right to a job, the right to form and join trade unions, the right to rest, leisure and a standard of living adequate for health, well-being, food, clothing, housing, medical care, and necessary social services). FDR raised these issues in 1944, and while most advanced nations have adopted and implemented FDR's proposals, the USA continues to lag behind when it comes to economic and social security.

> *The one supreme objective for the future... for all the United Nations, can be summed up in one word: Security. ... Freedom from fear is eternally linked with freedom from want. —Franklin D. Roosevelt, 1944*

Finally, the record shows that when our government feels threatened, it can resort quickly to speech suppression, surveillance, jail, deportation, and torture. Like the rest of the Constitution's benefits, the extent of civil liberties depends on what the American people demand.

FUTURE

How the Constitution's report card will change in the coming years remains an open question. For the short term, the Supreme Court has been interpreting the Constitution as a safe haven for the privileged few; creating special rights for corporate profit and propaganda; and narrowing opportunities for voter participation so that unhappy voters cannot use elections to fix the system the Supreme Court has perverted.

Yet we should remember what history has shown us: in the long term, constitutions are shaped by a long term fight between two sides.

On the Left side, we have watched Levellers, Pilgrims, American revolutionaries, the Jeffersonian democrats, northern abolitionists, southern slaves, the Populists, the suffragettes, union advocates, civil rights activists, Vietnam protestors and anti-globalization demonstrators. These people—and more—have pushed for Madison's equality, Van Buren's democracy, Lincoln's working people, FDR's equality, and Eisenhower's liberty.

On the Right side, we have watched monarchists, theocrats, Tories, rich Federalists, slave drivers, slave owners, Bourbons, male supremacists, bosses, white supremacists, imperialists and neoliberal enthusiasts. These people—and more—have pushed for the heredity and opulence censured by Madison, the monarchical principle criticized by van Buren, the dollar principle deplored by Lincoln, the spirit of fascism condemned by FDR, and the military industrial complex feared by Eisenhower.

Can you tell there is more than one side?

Which side are you on?

What do you plan to do about it?

Don't be taken in
When they pat you paternally on the shoulder and say
That there's no inequality worth speaking of
And no more reason
For fighting
Because if you believe them
They will be completely in charge
In their marble homes and granite banks
From which they rob the people of the world
Under the pretence of bringing them culture
Watch out
For as soon as it pleases them
they'll send you out
to protect their gold
in wars
whose weapons rapidly developed
by servile scientists
will become more and more deadly
until they can with a flick of a finger
tear a million of you to pieces
—Peter Weiss, *MARAT/SADE* (1964)

Eternal vigilance is the price of liberty; power is ever stealing from the many to the few
—Wendell Phillips (1852)

WENDELL PHILLIPS

It's a Republic, if you can keep it. —Ben Franklin (1787)

FOR FURTHER READING

Bachmann, S. LAWYERS, LAW AND SOCIAL CHANGE (2012).

Bachmann, S. "Starting Again with the Mayflower... England's Civil War and America's Bill of Rights," 20 QUINNIPIAC LAW REVIEW 193 (2000).

Beard, C. AN ECONOMIC INTERPRETATION OF THE UNITED STATES CONSTITUTION (1941).

Beatty, J. AGE OF BETRAYAL: THE TRIUMPH OF MONEY IN AMERICA, 1865-1900 (2008).

Black, D. SOCIOLOGICAL JUSTICE (1989).

Carroll and Noble. THE FREE AND THE UNFREE: A NEW HISTORY OF THE UNITED STATES (1977).

Caute, D. THE GREAT FEAR: THE ANTI-COMMUNIST PURGE UNDER TRUMAN AND EISENHOWER (1978).

Cogan, N., ed. THE COMPLETE BILL OF RIGHTS: THE DRAFTS, DEBATES, SOURCES AND ORIGINS (1997).

Dinan, J. KEEPING THE PEOPLE'S LIBERTIES: LEGISLATORS, CITIZENS AND JUDGES AS GUARDIANS OF RIGHTS (1998).

Dudziak, M. COLD WAR CIVIL RIGHTS: RACE AND THE IMAGE OF AMERICAN DEMOCRACY (2000).

Duxbury, N. PATTERNS OF AMERICAN JURISPRUDENCE (1995).

Ellis, R. THE JEFFERSONIAN CRISIS: COURTS AND POLITICS IN THE YOUNG REPUBLIC (1971).

Ely, J. DEMOCRACY AND DISTRUST (1980).

Foner, E. RECONSTRUCTION: AMERICA'S UNFINISHED REVOLUTION, 1863-1877 (1988).

Forbath, W. LAW AND THE SHAPING OF THE AMERICAN LABOR MOVEMENT (1991).

Foucault, M. THE BIRTH OF BIOPOLITICS (2008).

Fraser, and Gerstle, ed. RULING AMERICAN: A HISTORY OF WEALTH AND POWER IN A DEMOCRACY (2005).

Goodwyn, L. DEMOCRATIC PROMISE: THE POPULIST MOVEMENT IN AMERICA (1976).

Hammond, Bray. BANKS AND POLITICS IN AMERICA (1985).

Harvey, D. THE ENIGMA OF CAPITAL (2010).

Hofstadter, R., and M. Wallace, ed. AMERICAN VIOLENCE (1970).

Horwitz, M. THE TRANSFORMATION OF AMERICAN LAW. 1780-1860 (1977).

Horwitz, M. THE TRANSFORMATION OF AMERICAN LAW. 1870-1960 (1992).

Hyde, L. COMMON AS AIR: REVOLUTION, ART AND OWNERSHIP (2010).

Johnson, C. THE SORROWS OF EMPIRE: MILITARISM, SECRECY, AND THE END OF THE REPUBLIC (2004).

Karp. W. THE POLITICS OF WAR: THE STORY OF TWO WARS WHICH ALTERED FOREVER THE POLITICAL LIFE OF THE AMERICAN REPUBLIC (1890-1920) (1979).

Kinoy, A. RIGHTS ON TRIAL: ODYSSEY OF A PEOPLE'S LAWYER (1983).

Kramer, L. THE PEOPLE THEMSELVES: POPULAR CONSTITUTIONALISM AND JUDICIAL REVIEW (2004).

McPherson, J. DRAWN WITH THE SWORD: REFLECTIONS ON THE AMERICAN CIVIL WAR (1996).

Miringoff and Miringoff. THE SOCIAL HEALTH OF THE NATION: HOW AMERICA IS REALLY DOING (1999).

Morris, A. THE ORIGINS OF THE CIVIL RIGHTS MOVEMENT: BLACK COMMUNITES ORGANIZING FOR CHANGE (1984).

Phillips, K. THE COUSINS' WARS: RELIGION, POLITICS & THE TRIUMPH OF ANGLO-AMERICA (1999).

Powe, L. THE SUPREME COURT AND THE AMERICAN ELITE, 1789-2008 (2009).

Posner and Sunstein. LAW & HAPPINESS (2010).

Rosenberg, G. THE HOLLOW HOPE: CAN COURTS BRING ABOUT SOCIAL CHANGE? (1991).

Sandel, M. JUSTICE (2009).

Smith, P. THE CONSTITUTION: A DOCUMENTARY AND NARRATIVE HISTORY (1980).

Sunstein, C. THE SECOND BILL OF RIGHTS: FDR'S UNIFIN-SHED REVOLUTION AND WHY WE NEED IT MORE THAN EVER (2004).

Teles, S. THE RISE OF THE CONSERVATIVE LEGAL MOVE-MENT: THE BATTLE FOR CONTROL OF THE LAW (2008).

Thompson, E. P. THE POVERTY OF THEORY AND OTHER ESSAYS (1978).

Weiss, P. MARAT/SADE (1970).

White, G. E. THE MARSHALL COURT AND CULTURAL CHANGE, 1815-1835 (1991).

Wilkinson, R. UNHEALTHY SOCIETIES: THE AFFLICTIONS OF INEQUALITY (1996).

Wilkinson and Pickett. THE SPIRIT LEVEL: WHY GREATER EQUALITY MAKES SOCIETIES STRONGER (2010).

Zinn, H. A PEOPLE'S HISTORY OF THE UNITED STATES: 1492 TO PRESENT (2003).

THE U.S. CONSTITUTION

We the People of the United States, in Order to form a more perfect Union, establish Justice, insure domestic Tranquility, provide for the common defence, promote the general Welfare, and secure the Blessings of Liberty to ourselves and our Posterity, do ordain and establish this Constitution for the United States of America.

Article. I.

Section. 1.

All legislative Powers herein granted shall be vested in a Congress of the United States, which shall consist of a Senate and House of Representatives.

Section. 2.

The House of Representatives shall be composed of Members chosen every second Year by the People of the several States, and the Electors in each State shall have the Qualifications requisite for Electors of the most numerous Branch of the State Legislature.

No Person shall be a Representative who shall not have attained to the Age of twenty five Years, and been seven Years a Citizen of the United States, and who shall not, when elected, be an Inhabitant of that State in which he shall be chosen.

Representatives and direct Taxes shall be apportioned among the several States which may be included within this Union, according to their respective Numbers, which shall be determined by adding to the whole Number of free Persons, including those bound to Service for a Term of Years, and excluding Indians not taxed, three fifths of all other Persons. The actual Enumeration shall be made within three Years after the first Meeting of the Congress of the United States, and within every subsequent Term of ten Years, in such Manner as they shall by Law direct. The Number of Representatives shall not exceed one for every thirty Thousand, but each State shall have at Least one Representative; and until such enumeration shall be made, the State of New Hampshire shall be entitled to chuse three, Massachusetts eight, Rhode-Island and Providence Plantations one, Connecticut five, New-York six, New Jersey four, Pennsylvania eight, Delaware one, Maryland six, Virginia ten, North Carolina five, South Carolina five, and Georgia three.

When vacancies happen in the Representation from any State, the Executive Authority thereof shall issue Writs of Election to fill such Vacancies.

The House of Representatives shall chuse their Speaker and other Officers; and shall have the sole Power of Impeachment.

Section. 3.

The Senate of the United States shall be composed of two Senators from each State, chosen by the Legislature thereof for six Years; and each Senator shall have one Vote.

Immediately after they shall be assembled in Consequence of the first Election, they shall be divided as equally as may be into three Classes. The Seats of the Senators of the first Class shall be vacated at the Expiration of the second Year, of the second Class at the Expiration of the fourth Year, and of the third Class at the Expiration of the sixth Year, so that one third may be chosen every second Year; and if Vacancies happen by Resignation, or otherwise, during the Recess of the Legislature of any State, the Executive thereof may make temporary Appointments until the next Meeting of the Legislature, which shall then fill such Vacancies.

No Person shall be a Senator who shall not have attained to the Age of thirty Years, and been nine Years a Citizen of the United States, and who shall not, when elected, be an Inhabitant of that State for which he shall be chosen.

The Vice President of the United States shall be President of the Senate, but shall have no Vote, unless they be equally divided.

The Senate shall chuse their other Officers, and also a President pro tempore, in the Absence of the Vice President, or when he shall exercise the Office of President of the United States.

The Senate shall have the sole Power to try all Impeachments. When sitting for that Purpose, they shall be on Oath or Affirmation. When the President of the United States is tried, the Chief Justice shall preside: And no Person shall be convicted without the Concurrence of two thirds of the Members present.

Judgment in Cases of Impeachment shall not extend further than to removal from Office, and disqualification to hold and enjoy any Office of honor, Trust or Profit under the United States: but the Party convicted shall nevertheless be liable and subject to Indictment, Trial, Judgment and Punishment, according to Law.

Section. 4.

The Times, Places and Manner of holding Elections for Senators and Representatives, shall be prescribed in each State by the Legislature thereof; but the Congress may at any time by Law make or alter such Regulations, except as to the Places of chusing Senators.

The Congress shall assemble at least once in every Year, and such Meeting shall be on the first Monday in December, unless they shall by Law appoint a different Day.

Section. 5.

Each House shall be the Judge of the Elections, Returns and Qualifications of its own Members, and a Majority of each shall constitute a Quorum to do Business; but a smaller Number may adjourn from day to day, and may be authorized to compel the Attendance of absent Members, in such Manner, and under such Penalties as each House may provide.

Each House may determine the Rules of its Proceedings, punish its Members for disorderly Behaviour, and, with the Concurrence of two thirds, expel a Member.

Each House shall keep a Journal of its Proceedings, and from time to time publish the same, excepting such Parts as may in their Judgment require Secrecy; and the Yeas and Nays of the Members of either House on any question shall, at the Desire of one fifth of those Present, be entered on the Journal.

Neither House, during the Session of Congress, shall, without the Consent of the other, adjourn for more than three days, nor to any other Place than that in which the two Houses shall be sitting.

Section. 6.

The Senators and Representatives shall receive a Compensation for their Services, to be ascertained by Law, and paid out of the Treasury of the United States. They shall in all Cases, except Treason, Felony and Breach of the Peace, be privileged from Arrest during their Attendance at the Session of their respective Houses, and in going to and returning from the same; and for any Speech or Debate in either House, they shall not be questioned in any other Place.

No Senator or Representative shall, during the Time for which he was elected, be appointed to any civil Office under the Authority of the United States, which shall have been created, or the Emoluments whereof shall have been encreased during such time; and no Person holding any Office under the United States, shall be a Member of either House during his Continuance in Office.

Section. 7.

All Bills for raising Revenue shall originate in the House of Representatives; but the Senate may propose or concur with Amendments as on other Bills.

Every Bill which shall have passed the House of Representatives and the Senate, shall, before it become a Law, be presented to the President of the United States: If he approve he shall sign it, but if not he shall return it, with his Objections to that House in which it shall have originated, who shall enter the Objections at large on their Journal, and proceed to reconsider it. If after such Reconsideration two thirds of that House shall agree to pass the Bill, it shall be sent, together with the Objections, to the other House, by which it shall likewise be reconsidered, and if approved by two thirds of that House, it shall become a Law. But in all such Cases the Votes of both Houses shall be determined by yeas and Nays, and the Names of the Persons voting for and against the Bill shall be entered on the Journal of each House respectively. If any Bill shall not be returned by the President within ten Days (Sundays excepted) after it shall have been presented to him, the Same shall be a Law, in like Manner as if he had signed it, unless the Congress by their Adjournment prevent its Return, in which Case it shall not be a Law.

Every Order, Resolution, or Vote to which the Concurrence of the Senate and House of Representatives may be necessary (except on a question of Adjournment) shall be presented to the President of the United States; and before the Same shall take Effect, shall be approved by him, or being disapproved by him, shall be repassed by two thirds of the Senate and House of Representatives, according to the Rules and Limitations prescribed in the Case of a Bill.

Section. 8.

The Congress shall have Power To lay and collect Taxes, Duties, Imposts and Excises, to pay the Debts and provide for the common Defence and general

Welfare of the United States; but all Duties, Imposts and Excises shall be uniform throughout the United States;

To borrow Money on the credit of the United States;

To regulate Commerce with foreign Nations, and among the several States, and with the Indian Tribes;

To establish an uniform Rule of Naturalization, and uniform Laws on the subject of Bankruptcies throughout the United States;

To coin Money, regulate the Value thereof, and of foreign Coin, and fix the Standard of Weights and Measures;

To provide for the Punishment of counterfeiting the Securities and current Coin of the United States;

To establish Post Offices and post Roads;

To promote the Progress of Science and useful Arts, by securing for limited Times to Authors and Inventors the exclusive Right to their respective Writings and Discoveries;

To constitute Tribunals inferior to the supreme Court;

To define and punish Piracies and Felonies committed on the high Seas, and Offences against the Law of Nations;

To declare War, grant Letters of Marque and Reprisal, and make Rules concerning Captures on Land and Water;

To raise and support Armies, but no Appropriation of Money to that Use shall be for a longer Term than two Years;

To provide and maintain a Navy;

To make Rules for the Government and Regulation of the land and naval Forces;

To provide for calling forth the Militia to execute the Laws of the Union, suppress Insurrections and repel Invasions;

To provide for organizing, arming, and disciplining, the Militia, and for governing such Part of them as may be employed in the Service of the United States, reserving to the States respectively, the Appointment of the Officers, and the Authority of training the Militia according to the discipline prescribed by Congress;

To exercise exclusive Legislation in all Cases whatsoever, over such District (not exceeding ten Miles square) as may, by Cession of particular States, and the Acceptance of Congress, become the Seat of the Government of the United States, and to exercise like Authority over all Places purchased by the Consent of the Legislature of the State in which the Same shall be, for the Erection of Forts, Magazines, Arsenals, dock-Yards, and other needful Buildings;—And

To make all Laws which shall be necessary and proper for carrying into Execution the foregoing Powers, and all other Powers vested by this Constitution in the Government of the United States, or in any Department or Officer thereof.

Section. 9.

The Migration or Importation of such Persons as any of the States now existing shall think proper to admit, shall not be prohibited by the Congress prior to the Year one thousand eight hundred and eight, but a Tax or duty may be imposed on such Importation, not exceeding ten dollars for each Person.

The Privilege of the Writ of Habeas Corpus shall not be suspended, unless when in Cases of Rebellion or Invasion the public Safety may require it.

No Bill of Attainder or ex post facto Law shall be passed.

No Capitation, or other direct, Tax shall be laid, unless in Proportion to the Census or enumeration herein before directed to be taken.

No Tax or Duty shall be laid on Articles exported from any State.

No Preference shall be given by any Regulation of Commerce or Revenue to the Ports of one State over those of another; nor shall Vessels bound to, or from, one State, be obliged to enter, clear, or pay Duties in another.

No Money shall be drawn from the Treasury, but in Consequence of Appropriations made by Law; and a regular Statement and Account of the Receipts and Expenditures of all public Money shall be published from time to time.

No Title of Nobility shall be granted by the United States: And no Person holding any Office of Profit or Trust under them, shall, without the Consent of the Congress, accept of any present, Emolument, Office, or Title, of any kind whatever, from any King, Prince, or foreign State.

Section. 10.

No State shall enter into any Treaty, Alliance, or Confederation; grant Letters of Marque and Reprisal; coin Money; emit Bills of Credit; make any Thing but gold and silver Coin a Tender in Payment of Debts; pass any Bill of Attainder, ex post facto Law, or Law impairing the Obligation of Contracts, or grant any Title of Nobility.

No State shall, without the Consent of the Congress, lay any Imposts or Duties on Imports or Exports, except what may be absolutely necessary for executing it's inspection Laws: and the net Produce of all Duties and Imposts, laid by any State on Imports or Exports, shall be for the Use of the Treasury of the United States; and all such Laws shall be subject to the Revision and Controul of the Congress.

No State shall, without the Consent of Congress, lay any Duty of Tonnage, keep Troops, or Ships of War in time of Peace, enter into any Agreement or Compact with another State, or with a foreign Power, or engage in War, unless actually invaded, or in such imminent Danger as will not admit of delay.

Article. II.

Section. I.

The executive Power shall be vested in a President of the United States of America. He shall hold his Office during the Term of four Years, and, together with the Vice President, chosen for the same Term, be elected, as follows:

Each State shall appoint, in such Manner as the Legislature thereof may direct, a Number of Electors, equal to the whole Number of Senators and

Representatives to which the State may be entitled in the Congress: but no Senator or Representative, or Person holding an Office of Trust or Profit under the United States, shall be appointed an Elector.

The Electors shall meet in their respective States, and vote by Ballot for two Persons, of whom one at least shall not be an Inhabitant of the same State with themselves. And they shall make a List of all the Persons voted for, and of the Number of Votes for each; which List they shall sign and certify, and transmit sealed to the Seat of the Government of the United States, directed to the President of the Senate. The President of the Senate shall, in the Presence of the Senate and House of Representatives, open all the Certificates, and the Votes shall then be counted. The Person having the greatest Number of Votes shall be the President, if such Number be a Majority of the whole Number of Electors appointed; and if there be more than one who have such Majority, and have an equal Number of Votes, then the House of Representatives shall immediately chuse by Ballot one of them for President; and if no Person have a Majority, then from the five highest on the List the said House shall in like Manner chuse the President. But in chusing the President, the Votes shall be taken by States, the Representation from each State having one Vote; A quorum for this purpose shall consist of a Member or Members from two thirds of the States, and a Majority of all the States shall be necessary to a Choice. In every Case, after the Choice of the President, the Person having the greatest Number of Votes of the Electors shall be the Vice President. But if there should remain two or more who have equal Votes, the Senate shall chuse from them by Ballot the Vice President.

The Congress may determine the Time of chusing the Electors, and the Day on which they shall give their Votes; which Day shall be the same throughout the United States.

No Person except a natural born Citizen, or a Citizen of the United States, at the time of the Adoption of this Constitution, shall be eligible to the Office of President; neither shall any Person be eligible to that Office who shall not have attained to the Age of thirty five Years, and been fourteen Years a Resident within the United States.

In Case of the Removal of the President from Office, or of his Death, Resignation, or Inability to discharge the Powers and Duties of the said Office, the Same shall devolve on the Vice President, and the Congress may by Law provide for the Case of Removal, Death, Resignation or Inability, both of the President and Vice President, declaring what Officer shall then act as President, and such Officer shall act accordingly, until the Disability be removed, or a President shall be elected.

The President shall, at stated Times, receive for his Services, a Compensation, which shall neither be increased nor diminished during the Period for which he shall have been elected, and he shall not receive within that Period any other Emolument from the United States, or any of them.

Before he enter on the Execution of his Office, he shall take the following Oath or Affirmation:—"I do solemnly swear (or affirm) that I will faithfully execute the Office of President of the United States, and will to the best of my

Ability, preserve, protect and defend the Constitution of the United States."

Section. 2.

The President shall be Commander in Chief of the Army and Navy of the United States, and of the Militia of the several States, when called into the actual Service of the United States; he may require the Opinion, in writing, of the principal Officer in each of the executive Departments, upon any Subject relating to the Duties of their respective Offices, and he shall have Power to grant Reprieves and Pardons for Offences against the United States, except in Cases of Impeachment.

He shall have Power, by and with the Advice and Consent of the Senate, to make Treaties, provided two thirds of the Senators present concur; and he shall nominate, and by and with the Advice and Consent of the Senate, shall appoint Ambassadors, other public Ministers and Consuls, Judges of the supreme Court, and all other Officers of the United States, whose Appointments are not herein otherwise provided for, and which shall be established by Law: but the Congress may by Law vest the Appointment of such inferior Officers, as they think proper, in the President alone, in the Courts of Law, or in the Heads of Departments.

The President shall have Power to fill up all Vacancies that may happen during the Recess of the Senate, by granting Commissions which shall expire at the End of their next Session.

Section. 3.

He shall from time to time give to the Congress Information of the State of the Union, and recommend to their Consideration such Measures as he shall judge necessary and expedient; he may, on extraordinary Occasions, convene both Houses, or either of them, and in Case of Disagreement between them, with Respect to the Time of Adjournment, he may adjourn them to such Time as he shall think proper; he shall receive Ambassadors and other public Ministers; he shall take Care that the Laws be faithfully executed, and shall Commission all the Officers of the United States.

Section. 4.

The President, Vice President and all civil Officers of the United States, shall be removed from Office on Impeachment for, and Conviction of, Treason, Bribery, or other high Crimes and Misdemeanors.

Article III.

Section. I.

The judicial Power of the United States shall be vested in one supreme Court, and in such inferior Courts as the Congress may from time to time ordain and establish. The Judges, both of the supreme and inferior Courts, shall hold their Offices during good Behaviour, and shall, at stated Times, receive for their Services a Compensation, which shall not be diminished during their Continuance in Office.

Section. 2.

The judicial Power shall extend to all Cases, in Law and Equity, arising under this Constitution, the Laws of the United States, and Treaties made, or which shall be made, under their Authority;—to all Cases affecting Ambassadors, other public Ministers and Consuls;—to all Cases of admiralty and maritime Jurisdiction;—to Controversies to which the United States shall be a Party;—to Controversies between two or more States;— between a State and Citizens of another State,— between Citizens of different States,—between Citizens of the same State claiming Lands under Grants of different States, and between a State, or the Citizens thereof, and foreign States, Citizens or Subjects.

In all Cases affecting Ambassadors, other public Ministers and Consuls, and those in which a State shall be Party, the supreme Court shall have original Jurisdiction. In all the other Cases before mentioned, the supreme Court shall have appellate Jurisdiction, both as to Law and Fact, with such Exceptions, and under such Regulations as the Congress shall make.

The Trial of all Crimes, except in Cases of Impeachment, shall be by Jury; and such Trial shall be held in the State where the said Crimes shall have been committed; but when not committed within any State, the Trial shall be at such Place or Places as the Congress may by Law have directed.

Section. 3.

Treason against the United States, shall consist only in levying War against them, or in adhering to their Enemies, giving them Aid and Comfort. No Person shall be convicted of Treason unless on the Testimony of two Witnesses to the same overt Act, or on Confession in open Court.

The Congress shall have Power to declare the Punishment of Treason, but no Attainder of Treason shall work Corruption of Blood, or Forfeiture except during the Life of the Person attainted.

Article. IV.

Section. I.

Full Faith and Credit shall be given in each State to the public Acts, Records, and judicial Proceedings of every other State. And the Congress may by general Laws prescribe the Manner in which such Acts, Records and Proceedings shall be proved, and the Effect thereof.

Section. 2.

The Citizens of each State shall be entitled to all Privileges and Immunities of Citizens in the several States.

A Person charged in any State with Treason, Felony, or other Crime, who shall flee from Justice, and be found in another State, shall on Demand of the executive Authority of the State from which he fled, be delivered up, to be removed to the State having Jurisdiction of the Crime.

No Person held to Service or Labour in one State, under the Laws thereof, escaping into another, shall, in Consequence of any Law or Regulation therein, be discharged from such Service or Labour, but shall be delivered up on Claim of the Party to whom such Service or Labour may be due.

Section. 3.

New States may be admitted by the Congress into this Union; but no new State shall be formed or erected within the Jurisdiction of any other State; nor any State be formed by the Junction of two or more States, or Parts of States, without the Consent of the Legislatures of the States concerned as well as of the Congress.

The Congress shall have Power to dispose of and make all needful Rules and Regulations respecting the Territory or other Property belonging to the United States; and nothing in this Constitution shall be so construed as to Prejudice any Claims of the United States, or of any particular State.

Section. 4.

The United States shall guarantee to every State in this Union a Republican Form of Government, and shall protect each of them against Invasion; and on Application of the Legislature, or of the Executive (when the Legislature cannot be convened), against domestic Violence.

Article. V.

The Congress, whenever two thirds of both Houses shall deem it necessary, shall propose Amendments to this Constitution, or, on the Application of the Legislatures of two thirds of the several States, shall call a Convention for proposing Amendments, which, in either Case, shall be valid to all Intents and Purposes, as Part of this Constitution, when ratified by the Legislatures of three fourths of the several States, or by Conventions in three fourths thereof, as the one or the other Mode of Ratification may be proposed by the Congress; Provided that no Amendment which may be made prior to the Year One thousand eight hundred and eight shall in any Manner affect the first and fourth Clauses in the Ninth Section of the first Article; and that no State, without its Consent, shall be deprived of its equal Suffrage in the Senate.

Article. VI.

All Debts contracted and Engagements entered into, before the Adoption of this Constitution, shall be as valid against the United States under this Constitution, as under the Confederation.

This Constitution, and the Laws of the United States which shall be made in Pursuance thereof; and all Treaties made, or which shall be made, under the Authority of the United States, shall be the supreme Law of the Land; and the Judges in every State shall be bound thereby, any Thing in the Constitution or Laws of any State to the Contrary notwithstanding.

The Senators and Representatives before mentioned, and the Members of the several State Legislatures, and all executive and judicial Officers, both of the United States and of the several States, shall be bound by Oath or Affirmation, to support this Constitution; but no religious Test shall ever be required as a Qualification to any Office or public Trust under the United States.

Article. VII.

The Ratification of the Conventions of nine States, shall be sufficient for the Establishment of this Constitution between the States so ratifying the Same.

The Word, "the," being interlined between the seventh and eighth Lines of the first Page, the Word "Thirty" being partly written on an Erazure in the fifteenth Line of the first Page, The Words "is tried" being interlined between the thirty second and thirty third Lines of the first Page and the Word "the" being interlined between the forty third and forty fourth Lines of the second Page.

Attest William Jackson Secretary

done in Convention by the Unanimous Consent of the States present the Seventeenth Day of September in the Year of our Lord one thousand seven hundred and Eighty seven and of the Independance of the United States of America the Twelfth In witness whereof We have hereunto subscribed our Names,

G°. Washington
Presidt and deputy from VIRGINIA

DELAWARE
Geo: Read
Gunning Bedford jun
John Dickinson
Richard Bassett
Jaco: Broom

MARYLAND
James McHenry
Dan of St Thos. Jenifer
Danl. Carroll

VIRGINIA
John Blair
James Madison Jr.

NORTH CAROLINA
Wm. Blount
Richd. Dobbs Spaight
Hu Williamson

SOUTH CAROLINA
J. Rutledge
Charles Cotesworth Pinckney
Charles Pinckney
Pierce Butler

GEORGIA
William Few
Abr Baldwin

NEW HAMPSHIRE
John Langdon
Nicholas Gilman

MASSACHUSETTS
Nathaniel Gorham
Rufus King

CONNECTICUT
Wm. Saml. Johnson
Roger Sherman

NEW YORK
Alexander Hamilton

NEW JERSEY
Wil: Livingston
David Brearley
Wm. Paterson
Jona: Dayton

PENNSYLVANIA
B Franklin
Thomas Mifflin
Robt. Morris
Geo. Clymer
Thos. FitzSimons
Jared Ingersoll
James Wilson
Gouv Morri

The Bill of Rights

The Preamble to The Bill of Rights

Congress of the United States
begun and held at the City of New-York, on
Wednesday the fourth of March, one thousand seven hundred and eighty nine.

THE Conventions of a number of the States, having at the time of their adopting the Constitution, expressed a desire, in order to prevent misconstruction or abuse of its powers, that further declaratory and restrictive clauses should be added: And as extending the ground of public confidence in the Government, will best ensure the beneficent ends of its institution.

RESOLVED by the Senate and House of Representatives of the United States of America, in Congress assembled, two thirds of both Houses concurring, that the following Articles be proposed to the Legislatures of the several States, as amendments to the Constitution of the United States, all, or any of which Articles, when ratified by three fourths of the said Legislatures, to be valid to all intents and purposes, as part of the said Constitution; viz.

ARTICLES in addition to, and Amendment of the Constitution of the United States of America, proposed by Congress, and ratified by the Legislatures of the several States, pursuant to the fifth Article of the original Constitution.

AMENDMENT I

Congress shall make no law respecting an establishment of religion, or prohibiting the free exercise thereof; or abridging the freedom of speech, or of the press; or the right of the people peaceably to assemble, and to petition the Government for a redress of grievances.

AMENDMENT II

A well regulated Militia, being necessary to the security of a free State, the right of the people to keep and bear Arms, shall not be infringed.

AMENDMENT III

No Soldier shall, in time of peace be quartered in any house, without the consent of the Owner, nor in time of war, but in a manner to be prescribed by law.

AMENDMENT IV

The right of the people to be secure in their persons, houses, papers, and effects, against unreasonable searches and seizures, shall not be violated, and no Warrants shall issue, but upon probable cause, supported by Oath or affirmation, and particularly describing the place to be searched, and the persons or things to be seized.

AMENDMENT V

No person shall be held to answer for a capital, or otherwise infamous crime, unless on a presentment or indictment of a Grand Jury, except in cases arising in the land or naval forces, or in the Militia, when in actual service in time of War or public danger; nor shall any person be subject for the same offence to be twice put in jeopardy of life or limb; nor shall be compelled in any criminal case to be a witness against himself, nor be deprived of life, liberty, or property, without due process of law; nor shall private property be taken for public use, without just compensation.

AMENDMENT VI

In all criminal prosecutions, the accused shall enjoy the right to a speedy and public trial, by an impartial jury of the State and district wherein the crime shall have been committed, which district shall have been previously ascertained by law, and to be informed of the nature and cause of the accusation; to be confronted with the witnesses against him; to have compulsory process for obtaining witnesses in his favor, and to have the Assistance of Counsel for his defence.

AMENDMENT VII

In Suits at common law, where the value in controversy shall exceed twenty dollars, the right of trial by jury shall be preserved, and no fact tried by a jury, shall be otherwise re-examined in any Court of the United States, than according to the rules of the common law.

AMENDMENT VIII

Excessive bail shall not be required, nor excessive fines imposed, nor cruel and unusual punishments inflicted.

AMENDMENT IX

The enumeration in the Constitution, of certain rights, shall not be construed to deny or disparage others retained by the people.

AMENDMENT X

The powers not delegated to the United States by the Constitution, nor prohibited by it to the States, are reserved to the States respectively, or to the people.

AMENDMENT XI

Passed by Congress March 4, 1794. Ratified February 7, 1795.

Note: Article III, section 2, of the Constitution was modified by amendment II.

The Judicial power of the United States shall not be construed to extend to any suit in law or equity, commenced or prosecuted against one of the United States by Citizens of another State, or by Citizens or Subjects of any Foreign State.

AMENDMENT XII

Passed by Congress December 9, 1803. Ratified June 15, 1804.
Note: A portion of Article II, section 1 of the Constitution was superseded by the 12th amendment.

The Electors shall meet in their respective states and vote by ballot for President and Vice-President, one of whom, at least, shall not be an inhabitant of the same state with themselves; they shall name in their ballots the person voted for as President, and in distinct ballots the person voted for as Vice-President, and they shall make distinct lists of all persons voted for as President, and of all persons voted for as Vice-President, and of the number of votes for each, which lists they shall sign and certify, and transmit sealed to the seat of the government of the United States, directed to the President of the Senate; — the President of the Senate shall, in the presence of the Senate and House of Representatives, open all the certificates and the votes shall then be counted; — The person having the greatest number of votes for President, shall be the President, if such number be a majority of the whole number of Electors appointed; and if no person have such majority, then from the persons having the highest numbers not exceeding three on the list of those voted for as President, the House of Representatives shall choose immediately, by ballot, the President. But in choosing the President, the votes shall be taken by states, the representation from each state having one vote; a quorum for this purpose shall consist of a member or members from two-thirds of the states, and a majority of all the states shall be necessary to a choice. [And if the House of Representatives shall not choose a President whenever the right of choice shall devolve upon them, before the fourth day of March next following, then the Vice-President shall act as President, as in case of the death or other constitutional disability of the President. —]* The person having the greatest number of votes as Vice-President, shall be the Vice-President, if such number be a majority of the whole number of Electors appointed, and if no person have a majority, then from the two highest numbers on the list, the Senate shall choose the Vice-President; a quorum for the purpose shall consist of two-thirds of the whole number of Senators, and a majority of the whole number shall be necessary to a choice. But no person constitutionally ineligible to the office of President shall be eligible to that of Vice-President of the United States.

*Superseded by section 3 of the 20th amendment.

AMENDMENT XIII

Passed by Congress January 31, 1865. Ratified December 6, 1865.
Note: A portion of Article IV, section 2, of the Constitution was superseded by the 13th amendment.

Section 1.

Neither slavery nor involuntary servitude, except as a punishment for crime whereof the party shall have been duly convicted, shall exist within the United States, or any place subject to their jurisdiction.

Section 2.

Congress shall have power to enforce this article by appropriate legislation.

AMENDMENT XIV

Passed by Congress June 13, 1866. Ratified July 9, 1868.

Note: Article I, section 2, of the Constitution was modified by section 2 of the 14th amendment.

Section 1.

All persons born or naturalized in the United States, and subject to the jurisdiction thereof, are citizens of the United States and of the State wherein they reside. No State shall make or enforce any law which shall abridge the privileges or immunities of citizens of the United States; nor shall any State deprive any person of life, liberty, or property, without due process of law; nor deny to any person within its jurisdiction the equal protection of the laws.

Section 2.

Representatives shall be apportioned among the several States according to their respective numbers, counting the whole number of persons in each State, excluding Indians not taxed. But when the right to vote at any election for the choice of electors for President and Vice-President of the United States, Representatives in Congress, the Executive and Judicial officers of a State, or the members of the Legislature thereof, is denied to any of the male inhabitants of such State, being twenty-one years of age,* and citizens of the United States, or in any way abridged, except for participation in rebellion, or other crime, the basis of representation therein shall be reduced in the proportion which the number of such male citizens shall bear to the whole number of male citizens twenty-one years of age in such State.

Section 3.

No person shall be a Senator or Representative in Congress, or elector of President and Vice-President, or hold any office, civil or military, under the United States, or under any State, who, having previously taken an oath, as a member of Congress, or as an officer of the United States, or as a member of any State legislature, or as an executive or judicial officer of any State, to support the Constitution of the United States, shall have engaged in insurrection or rebellion against the same, or given aid or comfort to the enemies thereof. But Congress may by a vote of two-thirds of each House, remove such disability.

Section 4.

The validity of the public debt of the United States, authorized by law, including debts incurred for payment of pensions and bounties for services in suppressing insurrection or rebellion, shall not be questioned. But neither the United States nor any State shall assume or pay any debt or obligation incurred in aid of insurrection or rebellion against the United States, or any claim for the loss or emancipation of any slave; but all such debts, obligations and claims shall be held illegal and void.

Section 5.

The Congress shall have the power to enforce, by appropriate legislation, the provisions of this article.

*Changed by section 1 of the 26th amendment.

AMENDMENT XV

Passed by Congress February 26, 1869. Ratified February 3, 1870.

Section 1.

The right of citizens of the United States to vote shall not be denied or abridged by the United States or by any State on account of race, color, or previous condition of servitude—

Section 2.

The Congress shall have the power to enforce this article by appropriate legislation.

AMENDMENT XVI

Passed by Congress July 2, 1909. Ratified February 3, 1913.

Note: Article I, section 9, of the Constitution was modified by amendment 16.

The Congress shall have power to lay and collect taxes on incomes, from whatever source derived, without apportionment among the several States, and without regard to any census or enumeration.

AMENDMENT XVII

Passed by Congress May 13, 1912. Ratified April 8, 1913.

Note: Article I, section 3, of the Constitution was modified by the 17th amendment.

The Senate of the United States shall be composed of two Senators from each State, elected by the people thereof, for six years; and each Senator shall have one vote. The electors in each State shall have the qualifications requisite for electors of the most numerous branch of the State legislatures.

When vacancies happen in the representation of any State in the Senate, the executive authority of such State shall issue writs of election to fill such vacancies: *Provided*, That the legislature of any State may empower the executive thereof to make temporary appointments until the people fill the vacancies by election as the legislature may direct.

This amendment shall not be so construed as to affect the election or term of any Senator chosen before it becomes valid as part of the Constitution.

AMENDMENT XVIII

Passed by Congress December 18, 1917. Ratified January 16, 1919.
Repealed by amendment 21.

Section 1.

After one year from the ratification of this article the manufacture, sale, or transportation of intoxicating liquors within, the importation thereof into, or the exportation thereof from the United States and all territory subject to the jurisdiction thereof for beverage purposes is hereby prohibited.

Section 2.

The Congress and the several States shall have concurrent power to enforce this article by appropriate legislation.

Section 3.

This article shall be inoperative unless it shall have been ratified as an amendment to the Constitution by the legislatures of the several States, as provided in the Constitution, within seven years from the date of the submission hereof to the States by the Congress.

AMENDMENT XIX

Passed by Congress June 4, 1919. Ratified August 18, 1920.

The right of citizens of the United States to vote shall not be denied or abridged by the United States or by any State on account of sex.

Congress shall have power to enforce this article by appropriate legislation.

AMENDMENT XX

Passed by Congress March 2, 1932. Ratified January 23, 1933.

Note: Article I, section 4, of the Constitution was modified by section 2 of this amendment. In addition, a portion of the 12th amendment was superseded by section 3.

Section 1.

The terms of the President and the Vice President shall end at noon on the 20th day of January, and the terms of Senators and Representatives at noon on the 3d day of January, of the years in which such terms would have ended if this article had not been ratified; and the terms of their successors shall then begin.

Section 2.

The Congress shall assemble at least once in every year, and such meeting shall begin at noon on the 3d day of January, unless they shall by law appoint a different day.

Section 3.

If, at the time fixed for the beginning of the term of the President, the President elect shall have died, the Vice President elect shall become President. If a President shall not have been chosen before the time fixed for the beginning of his term, or if the President elect shall have failed to qualify, then the Vice President elect shall act as President until a President shall have qualified; and the Congress may by law provide for the case wherein neither a President elect nor a Vice President shall have qualified, declaring who shall then act as President, or the manner in which one who is to act shall be selected, and such person shall act accordingly until a President or Vice President shall have qualified.

Section 4.

The Congress may by law provide for the case of the death of any of the persons from whom the House of Representatives may choose a President whenever the right of choice shall have devolved upon them, and for the case of the death of any of the persons from whom the Senate may choose a Vice President whenever the right of choice shall have devolved upon them.

Section 5.

I and 2 shall take effect on the 15th day of October following the ratification of this article.

Section 6.

This article shall be inoperative unless it shall have been ratified as an amendment to the Constitution by the legislatures of three-fourths of the several States within seven years from the date of its submission.

AMENDMENT XXI

Passed by Congress February 20, 1933. Ratified December 5, 1933.

Section 1.

The eighteenth article of amendment to the Constitution of the United States is hereby repealed.

Section 2.

The transportation or importation into any State, Territory, or Possession of the United States for delivery or use therein of intoxicating liquors, in violation of the laws thereof, is hereby prohibited.

Section 3.

This article shall be inoperative unless it shall have been ratified as an amendment to the Constitution by conventions in the several States, as provided in the Constitution, within seven years from the date of the submission hereof to the States by the Congress.

AMENDMENT XXII

Passed by Congress March 21, 1947. Ratified February 27, 1951.

Section 1.

No person shall be elected to the office of the President more than twice, and no person who has held the office of President, or acted as President, for more than two years of a term to which some other person was elected President shall be elected to the office of President more than once. But this Article shall not apply to any person holding the office of President when this Article was proposed by Congress, and shall not prevent any person who may be holding the office of President, or acting as President, during the term within which this Article becomes operative from holding the office of President or acting as President during the remainder of such term.

Section 2.

This article shall be inoperative unless it shall have been ratified as an amendment to the Constitution by the legislatures of three-fourths of the several States within seven years from the date of its submission to the States by the Congress.

AMENDMENT XXIII

Passed by Congress June 16, 1960. Ratified March 29, 1961.

Section 1.

The District constituting the seat of Government of the United States shall appoint in such manner as Congress may direct:

A number of electors of President and Vice President equal to the whole number of Senators and Representatives in Congress to which the District would be entitled if it were a State, but in no event more than the least populous State; they shall be in addition to those appointed by the States, but they shall be considered, for the purposes of the election of President and Vice President, to be electors appointed by a State; and they shall meet in the District and perform such duties as provided by the twelfth article of amendment.

Section 2.

The Congress shall have power to enforce this article by appropriate legislation.

AMENDMENT XXIV

Passed by Congress August 27, 1962. Ratified January 23, 1964.

Section 1.

The right of citizens of the United States to vote in any primary or other election for President or Vice President, for electors for President or Vice President, or for Senator or Representative in Congress, shall not be denied or abridged by the United States or any State by reason of failure to pay poll tax or other tax.

Section 2.

The Congress shall have power to enforce this article by appropriate legislation.

AMENDMENT XXV

Passed by Congress July 6, 1965. Ratified February 10, 1967.

Note: Article II, section 1, of the Constitution was affected by the 25th amendment.

Section 1.

In case of the removal of the President from office or of his death or resignation, the Vice President shall become President.

Section 2.

Whenever there is a vacancy in the office of the Vice President, the President shall nominate a Vice President who shall take office upon confirmation by a majority vote of both Houses of Congress.

Section 3.

Whenever the President transmits to the President pro tempore of the Senate and the Speaker of the House of Representatives his written declaration that he is unable to discharge the powers and duties of his office, and until he transmits to them a written declaration to the contrary, such powers and duties shall be discharged by the Vice President as Acting President.

Section 4.

Whenever the Vice President and a majority of either the principal officers of the executive departments or of such other body as Congress may by law provide, transmit to the President pro tempore of the Senate and the Speaker of the House of Representatives their written declaration that the President is unable to discharge the powers and duties of his office, the Vice President shall immediately assume the powers and duties of the office as Acting President.

Thereafter, when the President transmits to the President pro tempore of the Senate and the Speaker of the House of Representatives his written declaration that no inability exists, he shall resume the powers and duties of his office unless the Vice President and a majority of either the principal officers of the executive department or of such other body as Congress may by law provide, transmit within four days to the President pro tempore of the Senate and the Speaker of the House of Representatives their written declaration that the President is unable to discharge the powers and duties of his office. Thereupon Congress shall decide the issue, assembling within forty-eight hours for that purpose if not in session. If the Congress, within twenty-one days after receipt of the latter written declaration, or, if Congress is not in session, within twenty-one days after Congress is required to assemble, determines by two-thirds vote of both Houses that the President is unable to discharge the powers and duties of his office, the Vice President shall continue to discharge the same as Acting President; otherwise, the President shall resume the powers and duties of his office.

AMENDMENT XXVI
Passed by Congress March 23, 1971. Ratified July 1, 1971.

Note: Amendment 14, section 2, of the Constitution was modified by section 1 of the 26th amendment.

Section 1.

The right of citizens of the United States, who are eighteen years of age or older, to vote shall not be denied or abridged by the United States or by any State on account of age.

Section 2.

The Congress shall have power to enforce this article by appropriate legislation.

AMENDMENT XXVII
Originally proposed Sept. 25, 1789. Ratified May 7, 1992.

No law, varying the compensation for the services of the Senators and Representatives, shall take effect, until an election of representatives shall have intervened.

THE FOR BEGINNERS® SERIES

AFRICAN HISTORY FOR BEGINNERS:	ISBN 978-1-934389-18-8
ANARCHISM FOR BEGINNERS:	ISBN 978-1-934389-32-4
ARABS & ISRAEL FOR BEGINNERS:	ISBN 978-1-934389-16-4
ART THEORY FOR BEGINNERS:	ISBN 978-934389-47-8
ASTRONOMY FOR BEGINNERS:	ISBN 978-934389-25-6
AYN RAND FOR BEGINNERS:	ISBN 978-1-934389-37-9
BARACK OBAMA FOR BEGINNERS, AN ESSENTIAL GUIDE:	ISBN 978-1-934389-44-7
BLACK HISTORY FOR BEGINNERS:	ISBN 978-1-934389-19-5
THE BLACK HOLOCAUST FOR BEGINNERS:	ISBN 978-1-934389-03-4
BLACK WOMEN FOR BEGINNERS:	ISBN 978-1-934389-20-1
CHOMSKY FOR BEGINNERS:	ISBN 978-1-934389-17-1
DADA & SURREALISM FOR BEGINNERS:	ISBN 978-1-934389-00-3
DANTE FOR BEGINNERS:	ISBN 978-1-934389-67-6
DECONSTRUCTION FOR BEGINNERS:	ISBN 978-1-934389-26-3
DEMOCRACY FOR BEGINNERS:	ISBN 978-1-934389-36-2
DERRIDA FOR BEGINNERS:	ISBN 978-1-934389-11-9
EASTERN PHILOSOPHY FOR BEGINNERS:	ISBN 978-1-934389-07-2
EXISTENTIALISM FOR BEGINNERS:	ISBN 978-1-934389-21-8
FDR AND THE NEW DEAL FOR BEGINNERS:	ISBN 978-1-934389-50-8
FOUCAULT FOR BEGINNERS:	ISBN 978-1-934389-12-6
GLOBAL WARMING FOR BEGINNERS:	ISBN 978-1-934389-27-0
HEIDEGGER FOR BEGINNERS:	ISBN 978-1-934389-13-3
ISLAM FOR BEGINNERS:	ISBN 978-1-934389-01-0
JUNG FOR BEGINNERS:	ISBN 978-1-934389-76-8
KIERKEGAARD FOR BEGINNERS:	ISBN 978-1-934389-14-0
LACAN FOR BEGINNERS:	ISBN 978-1-934389-39-3
LINGUISTICS FOR BEGINNERS:	ISBN 978-1-934389-28-7
MALCOLM X FOR BEGINNERS:	ISBN 978-1-934389-04-1
NIETZSCHE FOR BEGINNERS:	ISBN 978-1-934389-05-8
THE OLYMPICS FOR BEGINNERS:	ISBN 978-1-934389-33-1
PHILOSOPHY FOR BEGINNERS:	ISBN 978-1-934389-02-7
PLATO FOR BEGINNERS:	ISBN 978-1-934389-08-9
POETRY FOR BEGINNERS:	ISBN 978-1-934389-46-1
POSTMODERNISM FOR BEGINNERS:	ISBN 978-1-934389-09-6
RELATIVITY & QUANTUM PHYSICS FOR BEGINNERS	ISBN 978-1-934389-42-3
SARTRE FOR BEGINNERS:	ISBN 978-1-934389-15-7
SHAKESPEARE FOR BEGINNERS:	ISBN 978-1-934389-29-4
STRUCTURALISM & POSTSTRUCTURALISM FOR BEGINNERS:	ISBN 978-1-934389-10-2
WOMEN'S HISTORY FOR BEGINNERS:	ISBN 978-1-934389-60-7
ZEN FOR BEGINNERS:	ISBN 978-1-934389-06-5
ZINN FOR BEGINNERS:	ISBN 978-1-934389-40-9

www.forbeginnersbooks.com